You are the *Problem*
You are the *Solution*

By

Andy Holligan

ShieldCrest Publishing Limited

Shield Crest

ISBN: 978-1-911090-29-8
Second Edition

A CIP catalogue record for this book
is available from the British Library

MMXVII

Published by

ShieldCrest
Aylesbury, Buckinghamshire, HP22 5RR
England.

www.shieldcrest.co.uk

DEDICATION

This book is dedicated to everyone who has the desire to step out of their comfort zone and improve their life.
Congratulations!

You are doing what 95 percent of the population are not willing to do. I wish you well.

ACKNOWLEDGEMENTS

I would like to thank everyone who has ever helped me by sharing their valuable time and insights with me. I will be forever grateful. Thank you to every self help author whose words of wisdom have helped to shape my life. In particular Maxwell Maltz, author of Psycho Cybernetics, Robert Kiyosaki, author of Rich Dad, Poor Dad and the rich dad series of books. Shad Helmstetter, author of What to Say When You Talk to Yourself and Dr. Joseph Murphy, author of The Power of Your Subconscious Mind. Thank you also to the Almighty, not only for turning my life around, but also for the opportunity to write this book. And last, but not least, a special thanks to a very good friend; Irene Cameron, whose hard work, patience and endless nights of typing, helped make this book possible.

Contents

PROLOGUE

'Why I wrote You Are The Problem, You Are The Solution'

My mission is to help people to improve their lives. My life has changed dramatically since becoming involved in multi level marketing and starting to read self help books in 1995. I have never missed a day of reading since. As a result, I feel I owe it to people to try and help them. I believe that every normal human being wants happiness, success, wealth, good health, good relationships etc and probably much more. The key to all of this is what you feed your mind.

It is possible for every one of us to achieve our dreams, but only if we control what goes into our minds. That is non-negotiable. The irony is that our thinking can be our worst enemy or our biggest asset. That's why it's so important to take control- because your results in life will never rise above the level of your thinking. That was my main reason for writing this book. When someone says to you "You can achieve your dreams", do believe, or do you doubt? You see, it's that inner voice that causes us most of our trouble, but the good news is that your inner voice can be changed to work for you instead of against you. This book will show you how. Simply reading the book and then forgetting about it will not do you much good. To have a life changing effect, the principles must be put into practice on an ongoing basis. Then everything will gradually start to improve; your confidence, your self image, your relationships, your finances and much more. Opportunities will open up and the limits will come off, and you will realise they were fictitious and didn't have to be on in the first place. I wish you well.

CHAPTER ONE

The Mind and Your Self-Image

You are where you are right now in life because of what has gone into your mind. For some of us it's good news, and for others it's not so good. This book was written to give you hope. It doesn't matter if you are confident or lacking confidence, what experiences you've had, or what your situation, you can change.

Yes, that's God's gift to us all. Apart from free will, he gave us the power to control our minds and therefore, to direct our lives and control our destiny. One of the greatest freedoms we have is having the freedom to change.

The good thing about life is that it's very forgiving; you can choose to waste your life, to become involved in crime, to develop bad destructive habits, and the world will stand by and watch. Likewise, if you choose to make a success of your life, become wealthy, help other people, and develop good positive habits, the world will also stand by and watch.

The good news is, we get to choose. For most of us, our self-image is not quite as good as we would like it to be - unless you are in the top 5 percent of the population.

This book can show you how to change your life. The book will not do it for you; it will only show you how. You have to put it into practice.

Everything in life up until this point from the day you were born has had an effect on and has helped to form your self-image. Self image is a term used in psychology which means what you truly believe about yourself in your heart — not the exterior image you might display to your family or friends but the quiet inner voice, your own inner voice that speaks back to you in the form of your own thoughts. This is often referred to as your inner self-talk.

It Does Not Happen by Chance

A lot of things have helped to shape our self-image and our beliefs about ourselves and our environment. Our experiences have a massive impact on our self-image, but the important thing about experiences is not so much what happened but how we handled it, whether we reacted positively or negatively. If we reacted negatively, our self-image deteriorated and we were badly affected, but if we reacted positively, our self-image improved and we felt great. I cannot stress enough the importance of grasping this concept.

It's not what happens to us in life, it's how we handle it. We can't control what happens to us; we can only control our response.

I believe that for everything that happens to us in life, there is always at least one positive option. There is always a right or a wrong way to handle something. Sometimes there is more than one right way to handle something, but it's not always easy and usually takes courage. Don't worry if you don't feel very courageous just now, courage can be developed over time, and this book will show you how.

What Is Fear?

We first need to recognise what fear is. Fear is an emotion, and if it's an emotion that means it is inside our heads. It is not external or outside in the world, so to speak; it's in the six inches between our ears, and anything that's in our heads can be controlled. Some people might speak of a fearful situation, and although the situation might have caused us tremendous fear, the fear was not in the situation itself but in us.

This is not to say that fear is easy to overcome; quite the opposite is true. In fact, I think fear is the most debilitating and probably the hardest to overcome of all the negative emotions. Fear can paralyse us, fear can stop us doing the things we really want to do, and fear can ruin our lives. But it doesn't have to be that way. In spite of all this, we still get to choose how we respond. It is always a choice. What happens is, when we do the thing we fear, the fear disappears, but when we give into our fear, the fear controls our life.

It's important not to avoid situations because of fear because the only way you can build self-confidence is by experiencing things, and the only way to gain experience is to do the things you fear.

Each time you face your fears you gain some self-confidence, whether you perform well or not. In terms of self-confidence, it's either going to be an upward spiral or a downward spiral, depending on your response. It's much better to have tried and failed than never to have tried at all.

There is only one way to conquer fear and that is to take action. Without fear there can be no courage. Ralph Waldo Emerson said, "Do the thing and you will have the courage."

Small Things Matter

It's important to realise that we need to handle all situations positively, whether big or small. Even the act of apologising for something you've done wrong or saying you're sorry takes a certain amount of courage. Over time these seemingly small things accumulate, affecting your self-image along the way.

Once you start reacting positively to situations and events and forming new habits, even seemingly small events can become stepping stones to greater ones, increasing your self-confidence at the same time. Most changes that take place in our minds happen gradually, on a subtle basis. For example, if someone is depressed, nine times out of ten it did not happen overnight, although I know there will be exceptions to this— if something extremely tragic has happened, for example, the loss of a loved one or some other traumatic event— but most of the time it has been an accumulation of events over a period of time.

It's Okay to Be Afraid

Everyone experiences fear at some time or another. Fears are different for everyone. What might cause one person tremendous fear might not cause someone else any fear, although that person will have different fears.

There is nothing wrong with feeling afraid. Even soldiers in battle admit they're afraid, but they still act in spite of fear— that's what makes them brave. Courage is not the absence of fear but acting in spite of it. There are other negative emotions that will be covered in this book, but the key is to never to let any negative emotions make your decisions for you.

God Created You to Be Great

God created us all with the potential to be great— yes, everyone, and that means YOU. As Maxwell Maltz explains in his book Psycho Cybernetics, no one is superior and no one is inferior. We all have different strengths and weaknesses; that's what makes us unique. Sadly, people with inferiority complexes or poor self-images have accepted something negative about themselves and have believed it. The danger is that once you accept something about yourself which is negative, it can become a self-fulfilling prophecy, which ends up putting you in a vicious cycle that is extremely hard to break. For example, someone might say, "I'm running late as usual," or, "Every time I have an appointment I'm always late," and if a person keeps repeating negative statements like these on a regular basis, then after a while it becomes accepted as true by their subconscious mind and they shouldn't be surprised when they find themselves being late on a regular basis. In fact, since being late is now firmly entrenched in their belief system, they really have to be late in order to be true to themselves. The longer and more deeply ingrained the belief, the longer it will take to get out of, but it can be done. It all begins by taking control of your mind, which will be clearly explained in this book, giving you concrete steps to break out of negative thinking patterns and improve your life.

How the Mind Works

Our mind consists of two main parts, the conscious and the subconscious. As Dr. Joseph Murphy explains in his book, The Power of Your Subconscious Mind, the conscious mind is where we make decisions and logically think things out. For example, if you are counting something or if you decide to turn right instead of left, you are using your conscious mind, but this only accounts for about 10 percent of our minds. The conscious mind also decides what to reject or accept.

The subconscious accounts for about 90 percent of our mind and is by far the more powerful. The subconscious is the automatic part of our mind that has no reasoning of its own; it only obeys what the conscious mind tells it. The subconscious also acts upon everything you accept mentally, whether good or bad. It does not know the difference between truth or falsehood or the difference between a real experience or one vividly imagined. The subconscious is a goal-seeking mechanism that never sleeps and is constantly at work seeking to bring into physical reality whatever commands we give it. It takes every word we say literally and doesn't care whether we are joking or not.

It has also been proven that whatever we picture in our minds repeatedly is looked upon as a "goal" by our subconscious and it will draw us toward it in actual physical reality. This touches on visualisation, which is another subject in itself, but just to give you an example, worry is a form of negative visualisation. When we worry we are actually vividly picturing what we don't want to happen, and if we do this on a regular basis we can actually attract the very thing we don't want. On the other hand, people have used visualisation to help them achieve some extraordinary goals in life. Therefore, the subconscious can actually be "tricked" into success (or failure) depending upon what we tell it. As the subconscious does not argue back, we can use this to our advantage. We can also use it to help us create a new self-image.

The Difference between Conscious and Subconscious.

The subconscious mind can also be likened to a powerful truck being driven along the road. The driver, although small in comparison to the truck, gives the commands by deciding which way to steer it, which pedals to press, which controls to use, etc. He represents the conscious mind. The truck, although it cannot think for itself, is the actual powerhouse that does most of the work, and this represents the subconscious mind. This truck will gladly get us to our desired destination if we steer it properly and give it the correct commands; however, this same truck will also willingly take us off the road and into a ditch if we don't steer it properly or give it the wrong commands. Either way the truck doesn't care, it only obeys.

The subconscious is all-wise and knows things our conscious mind does not. The subconscious has stored in it every single event, experience, or thing that has happened to you since the day you were born, even if you can't consciously remember it. The subconscious never forgets and can also be likened to a huge storehouse that serves information up to the conscious mind when required. This is usually in the form of hunches or urges, but these hunches are not always in agreement with our conscious thinking and we usually think we know best. Have you ever been in a situation where you've had an idea or a difficult decision to make and you consciously thought it was a good idea at the time and you wanted to do it, but at the same time you also had this gut feeling telling you not to do it? You didn't know why, but you just had a feeling that you shouldn't do it, but you went ahead anyway? Did it turn out well? The chances are it probably didn't. The bad feeling you got was your subconscious trying to warn you of impending danger. Remember, your subconscious has been recording every single thing which has reached it through the five senses since the day you were born, and it gives all this back to you in the form of hunches and it knows best.

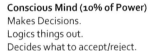

Conscious Mind (10% of Power)
Makes Decisions.
Logics things out.
Decides what to accept/reject.

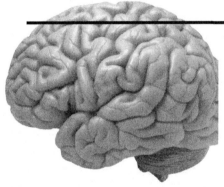

Subconscious Mind (90% of Power)
Controls our habits.
Seat of emotions.
Controls bodily functions e.g. heart beat, growth, pumping of blood.
Controls most of our body language.
Where hunches come from.
Attracts people, situations, events etc
Very responsive to input from 5 senses.
Beliefs.
Heals and constantly renews your body.
Can't tell the difference between truth and falsehoods.
Believes everything we tell it.
Doesn't know the difference between a real experience and one vividly imagined.

It is my personal view that the subconscious mind is linked to a Higher Power and is always trying to do what is best for us. The sad part is that most people have their subconscious minds working against them and they don't know it. How sad it would be for a person to go through their whole life, their one shot on this planet, and never discover the benefits of utilising this great power. Apart from God Almighty, the subconscious mind has been referred to by scientists and psychologists as the most powerful force in the universe.

It's Never Too Late

It does not matter what your past is, what age or color you are, or what mistakes you have made up until now. From this point onward forget about the past and only accept good positive things about yourself. Have you ever noticed anything about the mental attitudes of people who have battled against and overcome life-threatening diseases? Why does one person make a miraculous recovery while another person dies from it? They both may be faced with exactly the same situation, but the difference is in their mental attitude. Most people who battle against terminal illnesses and overcome them refuse to admit defeat. They just won't give in. Even though they are faced with the same "facts" as the other person, they choose not to accept the facts. For example, there have been people who have had cancer and were told by their doctor that they only had a year to live. There have been people who have had a stroke and were told by their doctor that they would never walk again and would spend the rest of their lives in a wheelchair— only to defy these predictions and not only make an amazing recovery but go on to achieve good health. Granted, they may have used certain techniques, such as positive affirmations, visualisation, or the miraculous power of prayer, but their attitude was one of faith that they would get better instead of expecting to get worse.

But some people may say, "You've got to face the facts, you're not being realistic," and in a way, they're right. We are not being realistic, but sometimes being realistic doesn't get us anywhere; sometimes being realistic isn't going to get us what we want. At the same time, bear in mind that you have the freedom to choose your mental attitude; that is your choice and your privilege. Although your conscious mind may know the facts, the subconscious part of your mind doesn't care about facts. It responds to what you believe, even if what you believe is contrary to the truth. This is an amazing law of the mind which few people understand.

The Power of Belief

You've probably heard about the use of placebos. These are only sugar pills, instead of active drugs. Lots of experiments have been done using these pills. Many patients who were actually ill were given placebos by their physician and were told they were real drugs and that they would get better after taking them. In many cases the patients got better, obviously not knowing that they had only taken sugar pills.

So why did they get better? The reason they got better was because of belief, and not because of the sugar pills. They believed wholeheartedly that they had taken real drugs, which would make them better, and because they believed, their sub-conscious mind responded and a healing took place. That is how powerful belief is.

Remember that your subconscious is linked to your immune system and controls about 90 percent of all your bodily functions including the healing process and the constant renewal of every cell in your body. You need to be very careful what information you feed into your subconscious as it will respond accordingly. It will accept harmful or destructive suggestions just as quickly as it will accept good, positive suggestions.

So my advice is do not accept about yourself that which you do not want to be true, as this will become your reality.

Friend or Foe ?

If we are not careful how we program our minds, our sub-conscious can work against us in many ways, without us realis-ing it. Negative emotions, the words we speak, the habits we have, and our beliefs, can all be contributing factors. If a lot of these things are negative or false then our subconscious will be working against us. What we want to do is make our subconscious a friend instead of an enemy and get this great powerhouse working for us instead of against us. Someone once said, "If you had a friend who talked to you, the way you talk to you, you'd get rid of that friend."

The trouble is, we humans form negative habits over our life-times and they are not easy to break, but with some practice and pa-tience they can be broken and replaced by good positive habits. As the subconscious is a creature of habit, it resists and resents any change. If, for example, you have told yourself for years that you are inferior to other people, the longer you have held the belief, the more deeply ingrained it will be in your subconscious thinking pat-terns, and your subconscious will quite gladly go along with this and will resist any information that contradicts this belief. What we need to do is take control of our minds by giving it the right information. The subconscious is able to be directed and is very susceptible to the words we speak. As Shad Helmstetter explains in his book What to Say When You Talk to Yourself, the subconscious mind can be likened to a cassette tape, that can be recorded over or taped over at any time, just as you can re-record new music on top of old music on a cassette tape, thus eliminating all previous recordings.

Fight Thoughts with Words

Most people vastly underestimate the power of words. Your words control your life whether you like it or not or believe it or not. The Bible tells us, "The tongue has the power of life and death" (Prov. 18:21).

Words are more powerful than conscious thoughts. What we need to do is break this negative thought pattern with spoken words, as spoken words immediately affect the subconscious mind and will override conscious thoughts. If this negative thought pattern is deep rooted and long held, the subconscious will resist these words to begin with but, if you persist, the subconscious will gradually start to accept these new commands.

Affirmations

It is very difficult to combat conscious thoughts with conscious thoughts; it usually doesn't get us very far and drains away our energy. What you need to do is speak words out loud to yourself called affirmations. An affirmation could be about anything you choose, but I recommend sitting down with a pen and paper and listing the areas you feel weak in and would like to change. For example, if you did not like speaking in public or felt nervous or had performed badly at it, your affirmation could be: "I love speaking in public. I enjoy doing it and look forward to it." Even though you may feel it isn't true just now, it doesn't matter, do it anyway. Remember, the key is to say what you want to be true, not necessarily what is true, and once your subconscious finally accepts these new instructions, you will find that your behaviour will change and you will start to perform differently without any conscious effort.

The key to affirmations is twofold:

(PROBLEM)

(1) IDENTIFY EXACTLY WHAT THE PROBLEM IS:
* I don't like speaking in public because I feel inferior

(AFFIRMATION)

(2) AFFIRM THE OPPOSITE
* I love speaking in public
* I look forward to it, I'm as good as anyone else

These positive words will flush out the negative thoughts if you persist in doing this long enough. You could even read out a list of affirmations for different problem areas on a daily basis to yourself.

How Often Should I Do This?

You need to do it every day. I recommend at least twice a day, once in the morning and once at night, preferably just before going to bed. Doing this first thing in the morning will set you up in a positive frame of mind for the day ahead, and affirming last thing at night will help flush out any negative thoughts which may have accumulated during the day. Affirmations can be used more often if you want, at any time, whenever you desire to use them.

How to Affirm

Once you have written down the affirmations you wish to use, make sure there are no other distractions (TV, children, pets, music, or anything that could divert your attention). You want to give 100 percent of your attention for these brief few moments to imagining what you are saying is true. For example, you might want to use an affirmation to become wealthy, such as: "Business is booming. Things are going great, and I'm getting richer every day." As you speak these words, picture it in your mind's eye, as if it were real just now. This will make it more real to your subconscious, which picks up this new image of you and will seek to bring it into reality.

As Shad Helmstetter states in his book What to Say When You Talk to Yourself, affirmations must be positively stated and in the present tense, What we mean by positively stated is that you can have two different sentences which mean exactly the same thing, but one is stated positively and one negatively. For example, you could say, "I must not forget to pick that up tomorrow," or you could say, "I must remember to pick that up tomorrow." They both mean the same thing, but one sentence included a negative word (forget), and one included a positive word (remember).

The way the subconscious works is it remembers or absorbs more vividly the main words or big words in a sentence. It doesn't really pay much attention to the smaller words such as if, and, but, etc and it doesn't really care much about the fact that you said "must not forget." The word forget has the most feeling to it, and this is what will stick or make an impression on the subconscious mind. Remember that the key to impressing something upon the subconscious mind is emotion. The stronger or more intense the emotion, the bigger the impact it will have on the subconscious mind.

In the Present Tense

It is important to use affirmations in the present tense. It would make no sense, for example, to say "I was wealthy." That would be foolish and would indicate to our subconscious that we are no longer wealthy.

And we do not really want to speak affirmations in the future tense either, because this would indicate to our subconscious that it has not yet happened and that we are not wealthy just now. We always want to speak affirmations in the present tense and say "I am wealthy," or, in the example I just used, "business is booming," not has boomed or will boom but "is booming." "Things are going great and I'm getting richer every day." Although that is a positive affirmation, it is best to be as specific as possible and state the actual amount of money you want to make. For example, "I am now making (amount) per year."

It doesn't matter if you are not actually making this amount when you say this. Just persist anyway because the subconscious will still take it as a command and will immediately go to work to devise ways of bringing it about, or it will provide you with opportunities to bring it about.

Remember, the subconscious has no choice but to feed off the information you put to it. That's all it can feed off— much like how a computer works: garbage in, garbage out, good stuff in, good stuff out. Someone once said; "The mind is its own place and can make a heaven of hell or a hell of heaven."

How Long Do I Need to Do This For?

It will vary for everyone. There is no set time frame for using affirmations; everyone's situation is different and unique. For example, if you are using affirmations to build self-worth or to restore self-confidence, then how long you need to do it will depend on how you feel about yourself just now and what kind of experiences you've had. The worse you feel about yourself, the worse the experiences you've had, or the more your self-confidence has been shattered, then the longer you will probably need to use the affirmations to get to a point where you begin to feel confident again. At the end of the day, you really have to decide for yourself how long you wish to use them. Bear in mind that the reason for using affirmations is to give new direction or a new way of thinking to your subconscious mind. Once you feel your subconscious has finally accepted what you are affirming and it has become a permanent way of thinking, you may decide that you no longer need to use that particular affirmation. Don't expect this change to happen overnight. You've got to be patient. How long have you been the way you are? For some people it's years, for others it's most of their lives; so don't worry, you're not alone. The negative experiences you've had probably happened over a long period of time, so you can't possibly expect to solve them quickly either.

First Person or Third Person?

There are different types of affirmations, such as first person or third person affirmations. First person affirmations are when you talk directly to yourself. For example, if you were using an affirmation to help you improve your public speaking abilities, you might say "I am confident and enthusiastic when speaking in public." Third person affirmation is when you talk out loud directly to yourself, but you act as if it is someone else who is saying it. For example, suppose your name was Fred and at the moment you were saying "I am confident and enthusiastic when speaking in public" (first person). Instead you might want to say "Hey, Fred, you really are confident and enthusiastic when you're speaking in public. I've noticed a big difference in you" (third person), as if someone else has just given you a compliment.

This third person type of affirmation is particularly effective if you've been used to a lot of put downs and criticism from other people. Your subconscious genuinely thinks you've just been given a compliment, and it has a powerful effect on you because you are not used to getting compliments. It's also important that you include your name when using third person affirmations as this conveys a very definite and powerful message to your subconscious that it is actually someone else who is doing the talking.

Someone who has not had much criticism from other people may prefer to use first person affirmations. This is not a case of a right or a wrong way, they are just different. One is as good as the other, and you just need to work out what feels best for you, or you may even want to use a combination of both.

All Words Are Affirmations

It is important to remember that, in a sense, all words are affirmations. For example, if you were using a list of affirmations every morning and last thing at night but were speaking a whole load of negative words during the day, you would be undoing all the good you had done. Your subconscious will act upon every word you say, not just the affirmations, so it is important that your words and your actions backup what you are affirming, morning and night.

The reason I say actions as well as words is that actions do speak louder than words — you've probably heard that saying many times.

Just as affirmations will override and direct your inner self-talk, so will your actions override and direct your inner self-talk, except your actions have a more powerful effect. Suppose you were using affirmations to help you become a more generous and thoughtful person and had been affirming this morning and night for several weeks. Your subconscious may well be starting to take this on board, but suppose when the time comes to be generous, you do the opposite. This negative action will override any positive self-talk of being a generous person and this new negative self-talk of being a greedy person will now dominate your thinking at a subconscious level.

Actions do speak louder than words (especially to your subconscious). Your actions or inaction at the end of the day will be more powerful than any spoken words regarding your inner self-talk.

Sometimes we find ourselves in awkward situations where someone has been complaining to us about something and we want to be polite and agreeable, but at the same time we don't want to take on their negativity and start complaining too. For example, you might be on your way to work in the morning and it's cloudy and raining, and your neighbour says, "What a miserable morning. Isn't it terrible?" Although the weather might not be good, if you were to repeat the words "miserable" and "terrible," they have the most emotion attached to them and would therefore make the most impact on your subconscious mind. You don't want to be disagreeable, but you could agree with them in a positive way by saying, "Yes it could be brighter!" The word "brighter" has the most emotion attached to it, and this is what will impact your subconscious mind the most.

Here are some examples of affirmations you could use relating to different topics. Remember, these are only examples and affirmations can be about anything you choose. A word of warning: Affirmations should only be used for good purposes— that means your own good and the good of other people— any attempt to use them in a negative way will surely backfire on you in one way or another.

Wellbeing

Every day I'm getting fitter and stronger.

My strength and speed are unlimited.

I am strong, healthy, and energetic.

My thoughts and emotions are positive, which brings health to my body and happiness to my life.

I was born to win.

Business

Everyone wants to do business with me.

I am the top salesman in my field.

My income doubles or trebles every year.

I now have time and money freedom.

Business is great and I get new contracts every day.

I am now making (amount) every year.

Relationships

I get on well with everyone.

I am a good listener and take a sincere interest in people.

People love me and look forward to meeting with me.

I love people.

The people I attract are friendly, honest, and sincere.

Spiritual

God helps and guides me in every way.

God protects me and cares about me.

God is my partner in success and I am divinely guided.

I can do all things through Christ who strengthens me.

With God all things are possible.

Habits

For the subconscious mind to accept new programming opposite to the way you've been thinking up until now, it will take a minimum of four weeks to notice any change, assuming that you're using affirmations every day. This is the way the subconscious works; it is a creature of habit, and you know the saying, "old habits die hard." So just because you've started using affirmations today, maybe even for the first time, don't think that a complete transformation of your subconscious mind will take place all in the same day.

A transformation will take place if you persist and you are determined, but it's going to take time and you need to be patient. Also, don't worry or be anxious about whether it's working or not, because these are also negative emotions. Instead, have the positive emotion of faith, faith that it is working. The changes that take place in our subconscious mind can sometimes be so subtle we ourselves don't notice until further down the road. Think about the leaves on a tree changing colour. Do you ever see a leaf changing from green to brown suddenly in the one day? Of course not, because it's a gradual process. So it is with your mind.

Another example of the subconscious taking several weeks to change habits could be the simple act of throwing waste paper into the bin. Suppose you've had the bin in the same place in your house for years and you suddenly decide to re-arrange the decor and you move the bin to the opposite corner in the room. For a while, when you decide to throw rubbish in the bin, you will quite frequently go to the original spot where the bin was. This is because your subconscious programming has not yet changed and the old original programming is still working away and controlling your habits. Even although your conscious mind "knows" where the bin is, it is the subconscious controlling your habits and not the conscious. After a while though, as you keep making errors and correcting them, making more errors and correcting them, each time you correct, this sends a signal to your subconscious mind, and through making errors and correcting them you are actually reprogramming your subconscious mind. Eventually the subconscious starts to accept the new programming, and once it has received enough of these "signals," the habit of going to the new location is formed.

The Real You

You were not born with a poor self-image or lacking confidence. These things have been "learned" as you went through life. As it says in the Bible, "For God did not give us a spirit of timidity but of power, of love and of self-discipline" (2 Tim. 1:7).

When you think about it, how many worried or depressed two-year-olds have you seen? How many two-year-olds have you seen with inferiority complexes? Probably none. The reason is that they haven't yet learned these things. Isn't it sad to see the smiling faces, the innocence and confidence, gradually disappear as they go through life? What happened? We ask ourselves. Where did it go? Can we get it back? The answer is yes, we can get it back, because anything that is learned can be unlearned.

The fact is, the "real you" has not vanished or disappeared; it is still there within you. It is a case of bringing it back out. It has been buried under layers of negativity gathered over years. Now please don't take this the wrong way, I'm not implying that you are a negative or bad person, but "life" happens to all of us.

We all have experiences, challenges, setbacks, hurts, etc., and these affect our self-image, our beliefs, and our outlooks, - a lot of which will be faulty or negative.

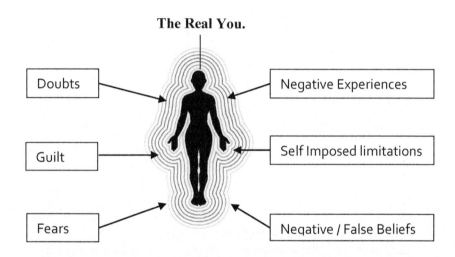

The Real You.

Doubts

Negative Experiences

Guilt

Self Imposed limitations

Fears

Negative / False Beliefs

Just to prove a point, if you look at some photographs of yourself taken when you were less than five years old, or even up until you were about seven or eight, what do you see? Do you look stressed out or worried in the photos? Do you look anxious or afraid in the photos? Is there much difference between then and now in terms of how happy you look? Well, understand that in these photographs is the "real you" God created, and God created you for success.

To "rediscover" yourself, it is going to take more than just affirmations; it's going to take controlling and monitoring what goes into your mind on a daily basis.

Your subconscious mind is affected by everything that reaches it through the five senses. That means what you read, what you listen to, who you associate with, what you do every day. You need to monitor what goes into your mind.

As someone once said, "The conscious mind is like the gatekeeper to the subconscious." Your conscious mind decides if you will read or not. Your conscious mind decides if you would rather read from a positive thinking book or from a newspaper. Your conscious mind decides if you will listen to motivational CDs or the radio. It's all down to you; it's your choice. No one can make these choices for you. You alone are responsible.

Self Imposed Limitations

Where do self-imposed limitations come from? They could have their origins in many areas. Sometimes they are passed onto us from other people, usually from family members or well-meaning but ignorant friends. Usually these people mean well and think they are protecting us, but the problem is that if they themselves have a poor self-image or self-imposed limitations, they in turn will pass these limitations onto us. For example, if you are presented with a challenge or opportunity of some kind and they can't see it for themselves, then they won't see it for you.

They may say things such as, "Yeah, it worked for that guy, but remember, you're not as confident as he is," or, "but he's got the gift of the gab, and you know what you're like at dealing with people." The problem is, sometimes we accept these opinions as true, and if they are accepted as true then every other opportunity or challenge that arises thereafter is viewed with these false beliefs in mind. We subsequently limit ourselves even further until we are caught in a downward spiral in terms of our self-image and our achievements in life. But who wants to be the product of someone else's negative thinking? I certainly don't. Do you?

Sometimes self-imposed limitations can be conjured up in our own minds without any input from other people. These are usually based on faulty assumptions about certain things as a result of a negative experience or our failure at something. For example, someone may have tried public speaking for the first time in their life and performed very badly and possibly even embarrassed themselves. As a result, they may come to the conclusion that they were "not meant" to be a public speaker and they may say certain things in conversation, such as, "I'm terrible at public speaking," or, "That just isn't for me." In other words, they base everything on that one single event, whereas if they had kept practicing and learning they could have improved and possibly even become a good public speaker. There are so many examples of people who were shy and introverted at one point in their lives but changed what went into their minds and, with a bit of hard work and practice, became excellent public speakers. Had they accepted those earlier "limitations," they would never have known what they could have become.

You need to realise there's a big difference between failing at something and being a failure. Just because you failed does not make you a failure. If that was the case then everybody who failed their driving test first time would be classed as failures in life, which just isn't true. Even the most successful people fail at some things now and again, but I'm sure they don't go around thinking, "Well, I did real badly there, so I guess I'm a failure." No, they probably still think of themselves as successful people but realise they messed up in a particular area and they may have to try a different approach until they do succeed. Self-imposed limitations are like a disease of the mind that needs to be gotten rid of if you are to be successful in life.

You could compare self-imposed limitations to the handbrake on a car. Normally speaking, with the handbrake off, this car can go anywhere, but with the handbrake on, it is severely limited. Are you going through your life with the handbrake on? Some people go for years with the handbrake on; others spend their entire lives with the handbrake on. Some people have multiple handbrakes and take them to the grave with them, never realising they didn't have to be on in the first place.

A good example of this was in 1954 when British medical student Roger Bannister became the first person to run a mile in less than four minutes. Up until then, everybody was firmly convinced that the limits had been reached and it couldn't be done. When he shattered these limits, or false beliefs, by running a mile in 3 minutes 59.4 seconds, there was a paradigm shift and people realised it could be done. When your beliefs change, results follow. Isn't it interesting how the following month this new record was further broken by Australian John Landy, who ran the mile in 3 minutes 57.9 seconds. The current fastest mile ever recorded was done in 3 minutes 43 seconds by Hicham El Guerrouj, in July 1999.

The important thing to realise is that even before these people had broken the myth of the four minute mile, the physical ability was within them all the time. The only change that took place was mentally.

"The only limits we have are those we place on ourselves." -
Bruce Lee

The Power of Emotions

Earlier we spoke about the fact that we cannot control what happens to us, we can only control our response— but have you ever wondered what controls your response? It has got everything to do with your emotions.

Most people underestimate or are unaware of the enormous part emotions play in our lives. Every day our emotions are constantly driving our behaviour, whether we are aware of it or not. For example, the fact you are reading this book means that you had the *desire* to learn something, for which I congratulate you. People buy birthday presents for loved ones because they *love* them. People buy lottery tickets because they *hope* they are going to win. People pray to God because they have *faith* in Him.

All day long our emotions are ebbing and flowing. Now this is all very well when our emotions are positive, but the danger lies in having negative emotions and allowing them to control our behaviour.

As Napoleon Hill states in his book Think and Grow Rich, emotions generally fall into two basic groups, positive and negative. The positive emotions are to be practiced and embraced, and the negative emotions are to be avoided. He also makes it clear that the only way to have positive emotions is to practice them. You cannot simply claim to "have" a positive emotion if your actions do not back this up. He states that positive and negative emotions cannot occupy the mind at the same time; one or the other must dominate. For example, if you were happy one minute then suddenly got angry, the emotions of anger and happiness could not co-exist, so the anger would take over and all the positive emotions would vanish. Obviously this works the other way round as well.

The minute we let negative emotions control our behaviour we are headed for trouble; in fact, they can give us a life of hell.

Now don't worry if you feel a little bit of negative emotions from time to time— remember, we are all human and none of us are perfect. What we can improve upon, though, is our behaviour. There is a big difference between feeling an emotion and allowing it to control our behaviour.

What I mean by that is, suppose you were at a party and there was a buffet and everyone was helping themselves. Suddenly you noticed a tray with your favourite cakes on them, and there were ten cakes left. Suddenly you got the urge (greed) to scoff the lot. What is important is not that you got the urge but what you actually did. Did you scoff the whole lot, or were you polite and maybe only took one or two.

If you were polite and you only took one or two, that is excellent; you fought the urge and won. You are on your way to taking control of your emotions, yourself, and your life. The journey of a thousand miles begins with a single step.

Our emotions can make us very happy or they can make us very unhappy. They also have a direct influence on our physical bodies as well as affecting our mental health. It has been proven that there is a very strong mind-body connection; therefore, if our emotions are positive we can experience excellent health, happiness, contentment, peace of mind, etc., but if our emotions are negative we can also experience misery, frustration, unhappiness, ill health, and even death.

There is even some evidence to show that negative emotions can actually contribute to the ageing process.

Our emotions also have a big effect on our immune system and our physical health. Negative emotions weaken our immune system and drain away our energy, and at times like this we are actually more susceptible to catching ailments than at any other time when our bodies might have otherwise fought them off. Conversely, if our emotions are positive, then even when people all around us are catching bugs, colds, etc., we can actually be in close proximity with those people and not catch these things because our immune system is stronger.

Controlling our emotions is probably one of the hardest things we can do because every day life challenges us and it tries us out. People try us out and we are faced with situations which we have to deal with while trying to maintain a positive attitude.

Napoleon Hill points out, in his book Think and Grow Rich that although there are lots of positive and negative emotions there are seven major positive emotions, and seven major negative emotions, these being the most powerful ones:

POSITIVE	Negative (To be avoided)
Desire	Fear
Love	Greed
Sex	Hatred
Romance	Anger
Faith	Revenge
Hope	Jealousy
Enthusiasm	Superstition

Sometimes we get urges to do something or to take some kind of specific action. Urges are different from hunches in that a hunch is usually like a flash of inspiration, or a sixth sense if you like, but an urge is like a motive to act or to do something, and we are not always sure where this comes from. Sometimes in life it can be the most difficult of times that bring out the best in people. I'm not saying that in ordinary circumstances there are not good people— good people are everywhere— but take for example the Blitz on London in 1940. Since the Luftwaffe had lost command of the air during daylight hours, Hitler's aim was now to break the will of the British people. Under the cover of darkness German bombers pounded the City of London and other major cities in order to terrorise the civilian population. Night after night people slept in air raid shelters and endured the bombing. Many civilians lost their lives. Some people were killed outright, others were made homeless, and some were trapped beneath the rubble. In spite of all this, they did not break the morale of the British people. In fact, the opposite happened; people drew closer together and performed acts of bravery, and the positive emotion of courage was the result.

Another example is the emotion of humour. Even in extremely negative circumstances, such as war, there have been times when this emotion was displayed. In World War II, the U.S. Air Force and her Allies were famous for decorating the sides of their aircraft with cartoons and slogans, even though many of these brave airmen would never return.

A lot of external or outside stimuli also affect our emotions.

Think, for example, about the different emotions you may feel when watching the news on TV, or listening to music, or seeing someone of the opposite sex, whom you find attractive. All these different scenarios, happening almost on a daily basis, activate our emotions. The reason I point this out is just to raise your awareness of your emotions, so that if anything does need changing, then you are better equipped to deal with it.

If an emotion is strong enough it can totally overwhelm our conscious minds and throw us into chaos. Take for example, the emotion of panic. Suppose someone who couldn't swim suddenly fell into deep water. The fear of drowning is so great and the panic so intense that there is no room for rational thought, thus demonstrating the power of the subconscious over the conscious. The same principle can also be seen regarding the emotion of guilt. If you have done something which you are feeling guilty about, you may try hard to occupy yourself with something in order to try to forget about it, but you can't forget about it. It stays with you and it won't go away. Guilt is a terrible emotion to have. It is like a fungus that eats away at the very core of your being and your happiness. The only way to deal with guilt is to simply stop doing what's making you feel guilty in the first place. Ask yourself if it's really worth it if it's going to make you feel this way. The answer is always a resounding NO!

CHAPTER TWO

Negative Emotions

FEAR (AND WORRY)

One of the best ways to control your emotions is to read from a positive thinking book, just a little bit each day. It doesn't have to be a lot, just a few pages every day, and over the long term this will have an enormous effect on you.

Fear and worry are very closely related; in fact, worry is a form of fear. If you are a worrier, I recommend you read How to Stop Worrying and Start Living by Dale Carnegie. In his book he explains that 92 percent of things people worry about never happen, and there is nothing we can do about the 8 percent that do happen, so why worry? Some people worry about things beyond their control such as global warming, a third world war, terrorism, etc., but what good does worrying do? It doesn't do us any good except to make us miserable and unhappy, so what's the point? Someone once said that today is the tomorrow that we worried about yesterday. In the book of Matthew we are also told not to worry: "Look at the birds of the air; they do not sow or reap or store away in barns, and yet your heavenly Father feeds them. Are you not much more valuable than they? Who of you by worrying can add a single hour to his life?" (Matt. 6:26-27). A lot of worry stems from what you focus on. Your mind has no choice but to focus on whatever you allow into it, but you decide what goes into it. So if you find yourself watching negative things on TV or even listening to them on the radio, you could be your own worst enemy. Why not turn the TV off or watch something positive and uplifting instead?

By worrying about something consistently, you can attract the very thing you fear. In the Bible it says, "What I feared has come upon me, what I dreaded has happened to me" (Job 3:25). This is because your mind is like a magnet. Your mind will always attract the physical counterpart of the most dominating thought held in the mind.

Fear has been described by some psychologists as False Evidence Appearing Real (F.E.A.R.). As mentioned earlier, fear is an emotion, and although the fear is very real to us, it can also disappear through taking action. I remember one time when I went swimming with some friends. At the pool they had four big tube-shaped slides which you went up the steps to and you could slide all the way down into a separate pool. At first we didn't know what they were like, because some were steeper than others and they all had different twists and shapes. We went down one or two of them and they were fine - no problem - had a good laugh. Then two of us decided to try this other slide. My friend went on it first and away he went. I just saw him disappear rather quickly. I went in next, and the next thing I knew I was travelling so fast it felt like a vertical drop. The water was rushing at me so fast I was coughing and spluttering. Foolishly, I must have had my mouth open, and it was over in a few seconds.

When I got out at the bottom my friend was standing waiting and was laughing, of course, and we both said, "I'm not going on that again!" So we both had FEAR of that slide. We still went swimming regularly after that and we still went on the other three slides but not on that one.

For months we went swimming but avoided that one slide through fear, but here's what happens: Your mind multiplies whatever you deposit in it. Now that's okay if it's something good, but if it's something negative like fear then it's not good. You've probably heard the saying, "Fear makes the wolf grow bigger than it is." It's just the way the mind works. For some reason, at a subconscious level, the mind seems to magnify things and the more time that passes by, the bigger they get until they become massive.

The point I want to make is this: Things do not get bigger in reality, only in our own minds. In effect, because our minds have blown something out of proportion, it would be fair to say it isn't real (false evidence). In other words, it is not accurate or objective reality, but it is still very real to us nevertheless (appearing real).

Anyway, getting back to the swimming pool, after about six months I learned that my friend had gone down this other slide (the one we had fear of) when I wasn't there. He said, "Yeah, it's great. There's nothing to it— I go down it all the time now." He said, "In fact, it's better than the other ones." Hearing his sudden change in attitude, I decided I had better do it as well. Obviously there were two reasons I thought I should do it: First, to be "one of the boys," and second, I wanted to find out what he had found out.

So the next time we all went swimming together, I went down this "other slide," yes the terror one, and to my amazement it was not as bad as I had imagined. In fact, when I came out at the bottom, I went back up the steps and went down it several more times, each time gaining confidence. This time I was a bit wiser; I kept my mouth closed and did not choke on any water. I held my breath for these brief few seconds, and I actually enjoyed it too. My friend said, "I told you it was better than the rest."

The point I want to make is this: Throughout all this, what changed? The slide didn't change. The only change that took place was inside our heads, which is proof of the fact that fear is mostly imaginative. I once heard a public speaker say, the worst things that ever happened to him happened in his own imagination, which is why fear often disappears through taking action. Action Conquers Terror (ACT).

Now this is just one example, but how many other areas could there be in a person's life where fear is holding them back? There are so many areas in our lives that can be affected by fear. Some people are afraid of what other people think. They might be presented with an opportunity to do something, but decide not to because of fear. They might "cave in" to peer pressure, which is fear of what people think, or they might have fear of what the opportunity actually involves.

You will never achieve greatly in life while you are allowing fear to control you. You need to break out of these "chains" which are holding you back. If you are suffering from the "but I can't" mentality or "you don't know my situation" mentality, that is okay. As you read on you will learn how to control your words and how to control your mind.

During World War Two, General Patton, in command of U.S. Forces, was asked if he ever experienced fear during battle. He replied, "Yes, I do experience fear before and during battle, but I never take counsel of my fears."

In the Bible there are countless verses referring to fear in which God tells us not to be afraid because He is with us. "Even though I walk through the valley of the shadow of death I will fear no evil, for you are with me (Psalm 23:4).

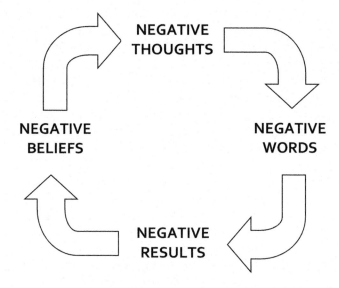

This negative cycle has to be broken.

Winston Churchill was quoted as saying, "When we are faced with adversity, if we stand firm and face it head on without flinching, we reduce the danger by half. If not, we double the danger, never run away from anything."

This is what the cycle should look like:

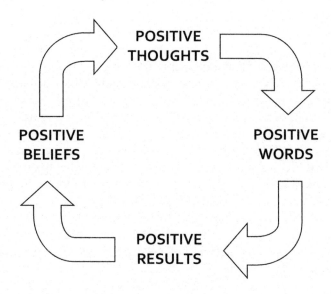

Another time that we can sometimes have fear is when we are faced with the "unknown." Unknown situations can cause us tremendous fear because what happens is since we don't know "the facts" our imaginations take over and run riot. For some reason we always seem to imagine the worst possible scenarios happening.

What ends up happening is we start reacting to our own imagination instead of the actual thing feared. We actually become afraid of our own thoughts. This can become terrifying if we do not learn to control our thoughts and to make our imagination an ally instead of an enemy.

Affirmations can help a lot in a situation like this, but if you are worrying or imagining the worst possible scenario happening, why not imagine the best possible scenario happening instead? You will find a lot of professional athletes, sportsmen and women, use a technique called visualisation. This is an excellent example of someone using their creative imagination positively so that it works for them instead of against them.

Before the event they are about to take part in takes place— suppose for example, it was a marathon— they would picture themselves clearly in their imagination winning the race. They would have done this repeatedly on a regular basis for weeks or months or in some cases years before the actual event took place. In fact, they would have done it so often and in so much detail that as far as their subconscious mind was concerned, the race had already been won.

The reason for doing this is that whatever we continually picture in our minds, our subconscious draws us toward. It's just the way the mind works. Psychologists and philosophers may disagree on some issues, but the one thing they all agree on is that we become what we think about most of the time.

Ex-world champion boxer Muhammad Ali was known to create what some psychologists call a "future history." This means that for a long time before the fight took place he would have shadow boxed the imaginary opponent in the privacy of his own room as much as a hundred times, so that when he stepped into the actual ring in real life, his subconscious already "knew" what to do and had already mapped out his actions, even to the point that he could predict in which round he would knock out his opponent.

That's why it's so important to imagine the best and to expect the best. Expectation is a very powerful force, which is constantly attracting things to us. We do not necessarily get what we want in life; we get what we expect.

GREED

Although I believe the vast majority of people are good, greed can still affect some of us from time to time. Greed is an emotion that is very destructive and can make us very unhappy, basically because it stems from being self-centred. The person who is greedy is not usually very happy and probably won't have too many friends.

Greed is actually an illusion and is very similar to the emotion of lust. The reason it is an illusion is because it is a trap. It is actually the devil's way of tricking us into having a life of lack, want, and misery.

Greed and lust are insatiable. Like a cat chasing its tail, it will never be satisfied. The irony of the whole thing is this: whatever we are greedy about or lust after takes wings and flies away and we have a lack of that in our lives.

I remember being in an internet café, I used to go to regularly for quite some time. It was reasonably priced and they also served unlimited free tea and coffee. Then one day it was suddenly taken over and was under new management. The new owner immediately raised the prices substantially and then started charging for the tea and coffee.

The result was that he lost a lot of regular customers. Now I'm not saying that prices shouldn't go up, because everything needs to go up from time to time, but if the motive is greed, then it's going to backfire. Proverbs 28:22 tells us, "A stingy man is eager to get rich and is unaware that poverty awaits him."

When someone is greedy, what do you think their state of mind is? Most of the time it is probably one of lack and shortage, which is why they are being greedy in the first place. Remember, the mind is always attracting or seeking to bring into reality the most dominating thoughts held in the mind. The result is that they end up with lack and shortage in their lives, and it becomes a vicious circle. I also believe that is one of the reasons why the poor get poorer and the rich get richer; it has a lot to do with how they think and their habits. The more they think about themselves in a certain way, the more they think about themselves in the same certain way.

So what is the answer? The answer is to become a giver, to be others–focused instead of self-focused, to go the extra mile instead of doing just enough. Instead of thinking what's in it for me, think, how can I help them? You'll be amazed at the change in the results you will get. A lot of people have fallen into the trap of thinking that the more they give to others, or the more they become others-focused, the less they will have left for themselves, so they hang onto every little thing they have. Actually the opposite is true. The more you give the more you get. Now I'm not saying you should give to get, but that's how it works. Think about it. If being greedy causes you to have a mentality of lack and shortage, then obviously to be generous must cause you to have a mentality of abundance.

I believe every normal human being wants the good things in life and the best life has to offer. Of course we would all like to be wealthy and travel where and when we want for as long as we want. We would all like to have the ideal partner, ideal relationship, etc. God knows we want these things and He wants to give them to us, but we must put Him first.

The Bible tells us in Matthew 6:33, "But seek first His Kingdom and His righteousness and all these things will be given to you as well." That means we must get our priorities right, because in life we are going to be tempted; and if we are tempted to put money or material possessions or personal gain before what's right, we shouldn't be surprised when we run into problems.

When you think about politicians today, not just in Britain but all over the world, how many of them do you think put the good of the country first and personal gain second? The answer is debatable, but I'm just pointing out that when we are faced with the prospect of more money or more power, it can easily cause us to fall into temptation or to compromise our values for the sake of personal gain.

If you look back at the history books and think about all the famous people who ever lived, the most famous ones are remembered for what they contributed to the world, not for what they accumulated. Thomas Edison invented the light bulb, Alexander Graham Bell invented the telephone, Robert Louis Stevenson invented the steam engine, and the list could go on and on. Great achievers such as them have made a lasting impression on mankind, and you and I still benefit from them today. How would you like to be remembered?

One principle that always holds true is that our state of mind is always reflected in the results in our life and our results are a reflection of our state of mind. As Denis Waitley states in his book, Seeds of Greatness, "As within, so without."

HATRED

The person who hates is usually very unhappy and will miss out on a lot of enjoyment in life as it is impossible to hate and be happy at the same time.

Hating actually harms you a lot more than it harms the other person; in fact, it doesn't usually hurt them at all. Why is this? Because it is "your" emotion. You are the one feeling it, and it's not serving you— it's holding you back. That's one of the reasons Jesus told us to "Love our enemies," not only because it is the right thing to do but because there's something in it for us too. That's one of the amazing things I've found out about God's commands. There is a hidden benefit to every command He gives us. The reason I say "hidden" is that it's not always obvious at the outset, so a lot of people never discover it. Only after putting it into practice does it reveal itself, and it has been my experience that the toughest decisions bring the biggest rewards.

The person who hates other people usually hates himself. It is impossible to love other people if you do not love yourself. Doubt is a form of self-hatred. To doubt yourself is to hate yourself. To believe in yourself is to love yourself. I don't mean to love yourself in an egotistical way or in a way that you look down on other people, but in a way that you are happy with yourself and you like who you are. The Bible says, "Love your neighbour as yourself" (Rom. 13:9).

Remember that whatever you give out will come back multiplied unto you. If you sow hatred, you will reap hatred. This does not necessarily mean that it will always come from the same source, but it will come back to you in one way or another. The Bible says, "He who sows wickedness reaps trouble" (Prov. 22:8).

Isn't it funny how we expect to be treated the same way we treat other people? If we show respect to other people then we expect to be shown respect in return. Likewise, if we hate other people, subconsciously we are expecting hatred in return, though we may not want to admit that; but that's how the mind works. Remember, expectation is a powerful force and is constantly attracting things to us, so doesn't it make sense to treat all people the way we would like to be treated?

You may think, but that particular person isn't important to me, so it doesn't matter if I hate him. Well, he may not be important to you, but you might reap hatred from someone else instead. So what is the solution to hatred? The solution is simple. You need to consciously change your attitude and decide not to hate. Ask God to forgive you for hating and decide instead to accept people for who they are and realise everyone is different and has a right to be different. If we hate a person because of their behaviour or the way they look, then we ourselves are at fault. We may despise their behaviour but we should not despise them.

One thing God always does is He separates the behaviour from the person. He may despise their behaviour but He will not despise them. We should do the same.

Hatred also affects your facial expression. While you are hating, you will repel positive people and attract only negative people. It's a well known psychological fact that "Who we are is who we attract." You will repel people who may have brought happiness and fulfilment to your life. You will repel opportunities, and it also makes you extremely narrow-minded and limits any creative thinking.

You also need to be careful with whom you associate. Remember, "Birds of a feather flock together." In other words, you become like the people you associate with. If you hang around with people who hate, then there's a very high chance you will end up hating. If they curse and swear, then there's a very high chance you will start to curse and swear.

People we associate with regularly are very influential at a subconscious level, probably without us even realising it a lot of the time. When I say "at a subconscious level," I mean things that take place in our minds automatically without us really thinking about it. For example, habits such as cursing or swearing, or any habit for that matter, often develop from other people.

People's attitudes influence us. People's views and opinions and the words they speak influence us. Why does all this influence us? Because our subconscious mind is on the job twenty-four hours a day and picks all this up, whether we are aware of it or not or like it or not.

People who hold grudges and resentment toward other people are also suffering from hatred. It may be something that happened a long time ago. It may be something someone did to you that offended you in some way, but unless you are willing to forgive and forget, then you're not going to move on either. In other words, it will be holding you back spiritually and psychologically.

Believe it or not, when you forgive a person you actually benefit a lot more than the other person. Why? Because once again it is your emotion, not theirs. It is you who receives peace of mind. Remember that negative emotions long held and deeply rooted can lead to all kinds of physical maladies or ailments.

Some people hate other people because of religion or politics or because they don't agree with them in some way, but realise, that other people have as much right to believe the way they want to believe as you have to believe the way you want to believe.

If someone has totally ticked you off or done something you think is absolutely wrong, instead of hating them, why not use humour and laugh at them instead or even feel sorry for them for being the way they are? At least if you do that your emotions will still be positive and it won't affect you. Remember, people who hate are small-minded people; it takes a bigger person to rise above something than it does to hate.

ANGER

This is probably one of the ugliest and most dangerous emotions that there is, yet every one of us suffers from it at some time or another. Anger is ugly because it's certainly not pleasant to see and dangerous because people don't think rationally when they're angry and may say or do things which they would not normally say or do. The trouble with that is that once you say or do something you regret, you cannot turn the clock back. You can apologise and try to make amends, but you cannot change the fact that you did or said something you wish you hadn't. Obviously it all comes down to maintaining self-control, which is easier said than done. Anger also wreaks havoc on your body, both physically and mentally.

A burst of anger or a fit of rage can totally spoil the rest of your day. It destroys all peace of mind and every ounce of positive attitude you might have had. It can cause people to avoid you, and it can raise your blood pressure. It also increases your level of stress. In fact, if you had a weak heart, a burst of anger could actually kill you. In short, this is an emotion you want to avoid.

What actually causes anger in the first place? A lot of the time it is simply the result of a bad attitude— not all the time but some of the time. For example, if you are waiting in line at the checkout of your local supermarket and find yourself getting angry, it could be your attitude that needs to change. A lot of people make the mistake of thinking it's the situation or the event, that causes the anger, but it's not. It's the belief or attitude about the event that causes the anger. If it was the event itself, then everybody waiting in line would get angry, but not everybody waiting in line will get angry because people have different beliefs and attitudes from each other.

Example of Bad Attitude:

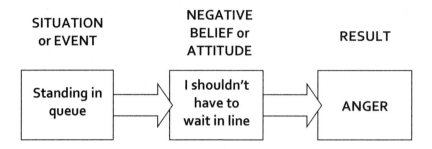

Example of Good Attitude:

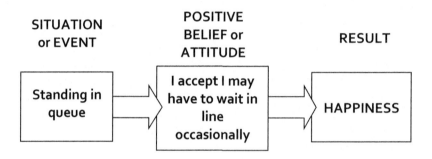

By changing your attitude or belief you also change your emotional response. Isn't it worth it, just to be happy?

Some people might say, "I hate waiting in line because I get so angry," obviously unaware their own attitude is the problem and not the event itself. Occasionally you might see someone "blow their top" and start shouting when most other people around them are perfectly calm. Obviously a person like this has very little self-control. Proverbs 29:11 tells us, *"A fool gives full vent to his anger but a wise man keeps himself under control."* Apart from anything else, getting angry isn't going to change anything, so what's the point? We might as well be happy about it.

Not all anger stems from a bad attitude. Sometimes in life things happen to us that are not our fault or beyond our control. We might get angry at an injustice or something unfair, and we are quite right to feel angry. Some psychologists call this "righteous anger." For example, if you had a colleague at work who suddenly shouted at you and spoke to you in a very rude manner for no apparent reason and put you down in front of other people, you would have a right to feel angry. The danger here lies in not venting the anger and bottling it up inside of you, which can lead to depression. Now you need to be extremely careful here, because this is where a lot of people lose control. *THERE ARE NEGATIVE AND POSITIVE WAYS OF LETTING ANGER OUT.* I'll just repeat that because it's so important. *THERE ARE NEGATIVE AND POSITIVE WAYS OF LETTING ANGER OUT.* It takes a wise man to know the difference and an even wiser man to put it into practice.

In this situation at work, a negative example of letting out anger — which I do not recommend — would be to physically attack them or to seek some kind of revenge. A positive way of letting anger out could be to have a word with them later on in private and to tell them exactly how you feel. Most psychologists agree that if you do feel "righteous anger" then you have to let it out in some way. As Robert Schuler explains in his book Self Love, either open up or blow up. But we must be extremely careful how we vent our anger. The Bible says, *"In your anger do not sin."* (Eph 4:26).

Isn't it strange how one negative emotion can easily lead to other negative emotions? For example, a person experiencing jealousy could very quickly suffer from hatred as well. Or a person experiencing revenge could very easily start to experience guilt and fear later on. These situations are very easy to get into but a lot harder to get out of.

Sometimes in life situations arise which cause us to have "righteous anger." You may have noisy neighbours who play loud music at three o'clock in the morning. These are difficult situations to deal with because we all want to solve the problem with as little fuss as possible, but usually there is some kind of legal action that can be taken and obviously this would be a positive way of releasing your anger. Just the fact that you are taking some kind of action to deal with the situation will help reduce your anger.

Some people in life complain about things constantly but never want to do anything about it. I've known situations where there have been "neighbours from hell," which ended up with some of the other neighbours starting up a petition. Some people signed the petition and some did not. Ironically, the people who did not want to sign the petition were some of the biggest complainers but said they did not want to get involved. The result was that nothing got done about it, so they may have ended up feeling anger not only at the "neighbours from hell" but also at themselves for not taking action. Most psychologists will tell you that anger turned inward can lead to depression.

The Danger of Inaction:

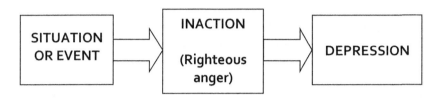

If your state of mind is already negative— you are in a bad mood or experiencing negative emotions— then it will much easier for you to be angered by someone or something than it would be if you were happy. We tend to see the world in a negative light when we are negative, and we tend to see the best in everything when we are positive. The same event or person that angers us when we are in a negative frame of mind might not bother us in the slightest when we are in a positive frame of mind. In a sense, "you are your world." As your emotions change, so does your perception. As your perception changes, so does your world. So if you want to change your world, you need to change yourself.

Another thing that has a negative effect on your psyche and your attitude is the use of swear words or 'cursing.' If something or someone has angered you and you curse or swear, even if only to yourself, it will reinforce an extremely negative state of mind within you and you will probably feel even more angry after swearing. The emotion you 'feel' when you say the words gets locked into your subconscious mind and becomes part of your psyche. So even if nobody else heard you swearing, it doesn't matter; your own subconscious mind heard you, and that's what matters. If, for example, the emotion of anger was what you were feeling at the time you said the words, even though the event has passed, the emotion of anger will still dominate your thinking for the rest of the day.

"Get rid of all bitterness, rage and anger, brawling and slander, along with every form of malice" (Eph. 4:31).

Anger at God

Some people get angry at God because they are going

through a tough time, or it could be because some kind of disaster has happened and they blame God. They might say, If God really loved me, He wouldn't let this happen to me," or "Why did He allow such a thing to happen?" Well, one thing is certain, and that is we will not know all the answers in this lifetime, but I do believe that one day "all will be revealed" to us. Even to His disciples, Jesus did not always explain things to them. He said, "You do not realise now what I am doing, but later you will understand" (John 13:7).

Another mistake we make is thinking God thinks like us, and we get mad at Him when things don't go the way we want them to. He tells us, *"For my thoughts are not your thoughts, neither are your ways my ways. As the heavens are higher than the earth, so are my ways higher than your ways and my thoughts than your thoughts"* (Isa. 55:8).

Obviously God works in ways beyond our understanding and we do not always know why certain things happen. We think He has forgotten about us, or that He doesn't care, but nothing could be further from the truth. Sometimes He does have to put us in painful situations to teach us lessons we need to know, but at the same time He promises us, *"I will never leave you nor forsake you"* (Josh. 1:5). God doesn't like to see us suffer, but sometimes that's the only way He can get through to us. Therefore we need to trust Him and have faith in Him. It would be unrealistic for us, with earthly thinking, to think an Almighty God who created the heavens and the earth would think like us.

REVENGE

Revenge is the emotion you feel when you stoop to the same low level as your enemy. Again, it is a small-minded person who contemplates revenge. Sometimes the person seeking revenge is suffering from low self-esteem; someone has wronged him or damaged his ego and he is seeking to "even the score" in some way.

The trouble with doing that is, firstly, it certainly won't make us any happier, although we may believe it will. Secondly, it has a negative effect on our self-image (who we believe we are). Thirdly, it can lead to other negative emotions such as guilt and possibly fear and worry. And last but not least we end up being just as bad as them for what we've done.

In short, when we seek revenge all we do is increase our troubles and get ourselves even deeper into the mess we are already in.

But not all revenge is due to having low self-esteem; sometimes in life bad things happen to us which are totally wrong or undeserved, and we feel angry and we have a right to feel angry. But remember, the emotion of anger usually precedes the emotion of revenge, and to seek revenge would be an extremely negative way of venting our anger (even in the case of "righteous anger"). An angry person with little self-control could easily fall into the trap of seeking revenge, and who knows where it could lead to?

PERSON WITHOUT SELF CONTROL

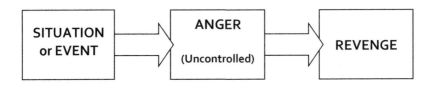

PERSON WITH SELF CONTROL

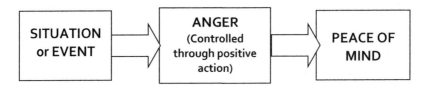

Obviously, in both examples, both people are angry. They could both be faced with exactly the same situation or event, yet the outcome is different, all because one person controls their anger and the other does not.

It is vitally important that you know the difference between what you can and can't control. For example, you are driving along the road and someone suddenly pulls out and smashes into the side of your car (SITUATION or EVENT), and although it was their fault, they deny they were to blame. You cannot control the fact that that just happened. You can, however, control your response— which will, in turn, affect the outcome.

Obviously a positive response (assuming no one was hurt) would be to keep calm, exchange details, and deal with it through legal channels rather than to start cursing and swearing or to seek some kind of revenge. This would be an example of controlled anger through positive action.

Revenge is really a case of taking the law into your own hands, but if everyone did that we would have anarchy and society would break down.

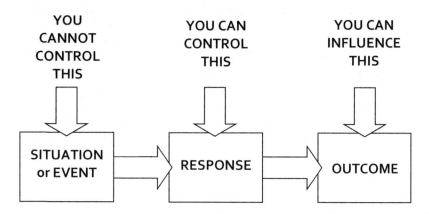

We need to have law and order to protect our citizens, but I'll be the first to admit that the law is not always fair. In fact, it seems as if everything today is geared in favour of the criminal instead of the victim. That may be true, but two wrongs still do not make a right. Politicians who take a softly approach to criminals or believe in too many rights for criminals are actually guilty of encouraging crime. Any psychologist will tell you that whatever behaviour you reward will either continue or increase, but there is still no excuse for taking revenge. Let's see what the Bible has to say about taking revenge: *"Do not repay anyone evil for evil. Be careful to do what is right in the eyes of everybody. If it is possible, as far as it depends on you, live at peace with everyone. Do not take revenge, my friends, but leave room for God's wrath, for it is written. It is mine to avenge; I will repay"* (Rom. 12:17-19).

Success Is Revenge

There are many people in life who have been presented with an opportunity of some kind or who have started out in a business of their own only to receive overwhelming criticism from either their family or "friends." Comments such as: "You've not got what it takes," or, "He'll never last," or, "It's just a phase he's going through," or "What makes you think you can do that?" Comments like these could anger some and could cause others to quit, while some may laugh it off. What would you do? What would your response be? Would it be controlled anger through positive action? Although some people, such as family members, may genuinely be trying to help you, other people may not want you to succeed. I know this sounds harsh, but it's true. Some people simply do not want you to get ahead of them and may try to steal your dream. They don't mind you having some degree of success, as long as it's not going to make them feel bad.

The best form of positive action (while controlling your anger) would be to go ahead anyway and become successful in your chosen field of endeavour, in spite of criticism or ridicule, because really, success is revenge.

JEALOUSY

Jealousy is a reflection of an inner state of turmoil within ourselves. Jealousy is actually a weakness of character and could be rooted in many things. It takes a strong character with a positive mental attitude to rid themselves of all jealousy. The person who rids themselves of all jealousy is much happier, has more self-control, and is able to rise above situations which could cause the average person to fall into the pit of jealousy. But who wants to be average? I certainly don't, and I don't believe you do either. The fact that you are reading this book shows you are already above average and you obviously have an above average desire to improve your life.

Jealousy can be seen in many areas in life. People are jealous of other people's goods or possessions. People are jealous when it comes to relationships. People are jealous of the rich. The list could go on and on.

A lot of jealousy within a person is rooted in low self-esteem. They believe they cannot have what the other person has, so they become jealous. Actually, the problem is in their own thinking. Their belief system is wrong. There is nothing one man can have that another man cannot. Once a person believes they can also achieve what the other person has achieved, they will no longer be jealous. Once again, the problem is in their mental attitude, and the only way to change that is by the books you read, what you listen to, and the people with whom you associate. This will be covered in more detail later in the book. Jealousy, unless gotten rid of, will be a barrier to your own success or whatever it may be that you want. Look upon jealousy as a barrier; look upon it as a brick wall standing between you and your dreams. You need to tear that wall down and eliminate it completely if you are to be successful.

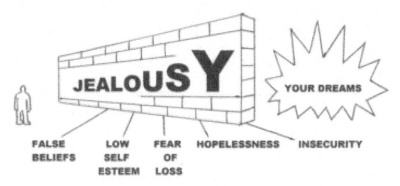

The reason jealousy will be a barrier to your own success is that jealousy often leads to criticism. Whatever people are jealous of they will criticise, and you cannot attract that which you criticise.

For example, some people may criticise a football player because of the amount of money he makes, but deep down these "critics" would probably like to have more money themselves so they criticise him. They say things like, "isn't that ridiculous," or "He doesn't deserve all that," yet some of these "critics" will go out and buy lottery tickets each week. Deep down these "critics" would love to have as much money as the football player but they just don't believe they will ever get it.

Now I realise not everyone is talented enough to be a professional football player, including me, but there are many ways to become rich. Don't think you have to become rich in the same way as the other person; he may be more talented than you at playing football, but there will be things you are more talented at than he is.

Remember, God has no favourites. God wants for you as much success and wealth as the next person. The Bible tells us, *"For I know the plans I have for you,"* declares the Lord, *"plans to prosper you and not to harm you, plans to give you hope and a future"* (Jer. 29:11).

The first step you need to take is to be genuinely happy for other people's achievements, congratulate them and wish for them even greater success in the future. As the Bible says, *"Rejoice with those who rejoice"* (Rom. 12:15), and obviously we will be happier people in the process. Ask God to provide you with an opportunity, because He will. God isn't going to tell us He has plans for us and then not answer us when we ask him.

Just the fact that you have changed your attitude from jealousy to one of rejoicing for others' successes sets you up in a positive frame of mind and will increase your chances of attracting opportunities. Think about it. If you were expanding a business and were looking to recruit one more person, who would you rather recruit? A person who is jealous and miserable or a person who is happy and fun to be around? I think the answer is obvious. If, for example, your goal is to make more money and to become wealthy, then it's important not to criticise people who are wealthy, because your subconscious mind links negativity with the object of criticism (money) and subconsciously you will repel it, maybe without even realising it and it'll keep you broke. Remember: if you desire something you don't yet have, you first need to recognize that it is good before you can attract it.

Another danger with jealousy is that it can lead to so many other negative emotions and sometimes negative actions. How many times have you heard of the "jilted lover" who takes some kind of revenge on their ex-lover? Or someone who is jealous of another person's possessions, so they steal from them (greed) or commit acts of "revenge." Before we know it, the whole situation is ten times worse than when it began.

Here are some examples

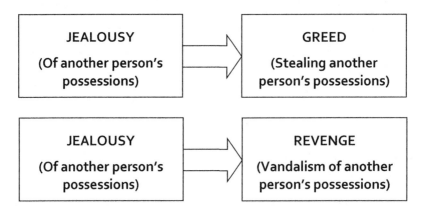

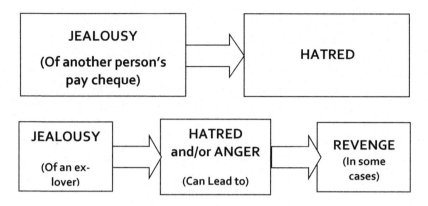

What a mess to get ourselves into! Don't you agree? Isn't it a whole lot easier to just not get jealous? You will certainly be a whole lot happier and save yourself a mountain of trouble. Apart from anything else, what a waste of energy. There is clear evidence in the Bible that negative emotions can damage your physical health as well as your mind: *"A heart at peace gives life to the body, but envy rots the bones"* (Prov. 14:30). It shouldn't surprise us when people with long held, deep rooted, negative emotions end up with all kinds of aches and pains and ailments. Don't be your own worst enemy.

When it comes to jealousy some people say, "But I can't help it," but the truth is they *can* help it. To say, "I can't help it," is a loser's statement, because the minute you say, "I can't help it," you have just given power to the situation. You have let the situation have power over you by allowing it to dictate how you will feel. Winners take control of themselves and take responsibility. They don't allow situations to have power over them. Winners also have a positive mental attitude, so don't allow a particular person or situation to steal your attitude.

Relationships

Jealousy in a relationship can lead to possessiveness. This is usually rooted in "fear of loss."

Because jealousy has many roots, we first need to identify what the root cause of the jealousy is. In this example it is fear of loss, although in some relationships it may be insecurity or some other reason. The person may fear losing their partner so much that they become possessive and "smother" them. Remember what we said earlier about letting negative emotions control our actions or our behaviour? The moment we do that we are headed for trouble, and if you let fear control your actions you can actually attract the very thing you fear. Some people think— (mistakenly) that if they are possessive with their partner they have more chance of holding on to them, but actually the opposite is true; the more possessive you are, the more chance you have of losing them. Why? Think about it— would you like someone to be possessive of you, quizzing you about every move you make, every person you speak to, and everything you do? Probably not, and sooner or later this person might get fed up with all this treatment and go off with someone else.

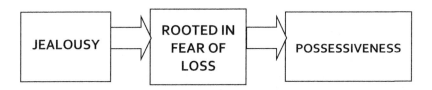

Most people I know want to have a happy relationship, but at the same time they also want the freedom to be able to live their lives. Obviously marriage is a different situation altogether, but for ordinary relationships I believe the old adage is true: "If you love somebody, set them free, and if they come back, it was meant to be."

The reality of the situation is this: The more freedom you give them, the more they will love you. By allowing them the freedom to "live," you actually increase your chances of holding on to them, although this may be hard to do for some. Have faith instead of fear; have faith that everything is always working out for your highest good. This does not mean that by allowing someone the "freedom to live" that they will always come back, but it certainly does increase your chances.

SUPERSTITION

Superstition is an emotion a lot of people suffer from today. In fact, superstition is commonplace and has probably been around for a long time and is just as widespread in adults as it is in children— though the reason some children may be superstitious is probably because they have been told about it by adults.

People may say its bad luck to walk under a ladder or good luck if a black cat crosses your path, but do people ever question where these beliefs come from? Probably not. They hear everybody else saying it and they've heard it so many times that they think it must be true, very seldom do they stop to question it. There are different types of superstitions, which can range from reading horoscopes to sorcery, witchcraft, or consulting the dead. Obviously some of these are more serious than others.

The Bible clearly condemns all forms of superstition, as it is based on falsehood instead of truth. It says, *"Let no one be found among you who sacrifices his son or daughter in the fire, who practices divination or sorcery, interprets omens, engages in witchcraft, or cast spells, or who is a medium or spiritualist or who consults the dead. Anyone who does these things is detestable to the Lord"* (Deuteronomy 18:10-12).

Don't get me wrong— I'm not saying that people like mediums or fortune tellers don't have powers. I believe they do. I know people who have been to them and I think their accuracy speaks for itself, but I don't think their powers are from God, otherwise God wouldn't condemn it. Remember that the devil also has powers and is very clever, although nowhere near as powerful or as clever as God. The devil knows our weak spots and is constantly placing things in our path to try to tempt us.

The devil also loves to play with our minds by lying to us, tricking us, and deceiving us. Remember, he was thrown out of heaven, and because he was not powerful enough to do anything against God directly, he decided to take out his wrath on people because God loves people.

"The great dragon was hurled down, that ancient serpent called the devil, or Satan, who leads the whole world astray. He was hurled to the earth and his angels with him " (Rev 12 v 9) So when Satan was thrown out of heaven, he took a third of the angels with him to earth and obviously these evil spirits are behind all the evil in the world today. You may be tempted to think, like I used to think, if God is so powerful, why does He not just get rid of Satan completely once and for all? Well He could if He wanted to and He will one day but not just yet. If God was to get rid of Satan just now, it would be a perfect world and there would be no such thing as doing wrong or evil, and there would be no temptation.

While this may sound great and the world would be the ideal place to be, God wants to test us. He gives us the free will to choose between right and wrong, good and evil, because if there was no evil, then there would be no test and there would be no point giving us commands, or judging us. But God tells us that one day Satan will be consigned to the abyss forever "And the devil, who deceived them, was thrown into the lake of burning sulphur, where the beast and the false prophet had been thrown. They will be tormented day and night forever and ever" (Rev 20:10) But as believers we are also reminded that one day there will be no more evil, and we will have eternal life. *"He will wipe every tear from their eyes. There will be no more death or mourning or crying or pain for the old order of things has passed away"* (Rev. 21:4).

Another thing that some people do is they trust in "good luck charms" to protect them, or they may put their faith in statues and material objects, but scripture tells us this is futile: *"Like a scarecrow in a melon patch, their idols cannot speak; they must be carried because they cannot walk. Do not fear them; they can do no harm nor can they do any good."* (Jeremiah.10:5).

You cannot be putting your faith in two different places. You either put your faith in God and shun superstition or you put your faith in superstition and shun God. I recommend putting your faith in God, as He is the only One who can give us salvation, but that is entirely your choice and you have the right to choose. This book is not written to convert you or to enforce my beliefs upon you, but it is written to reveal the Truth and although horoscopes may be at the milder end of the scale, they are still based on false prophecy. You may think, but I enjoy reading horoscopes, how can something as simple and seemingly harmless as reading horoscopes be wrong? Well, the important thing to realise is that it's not so much what you read that's wrong, it's what you believe that's wrong.

It's what you believe that God condemns, it's what or who you put your faith in that God condemns, and the danger is that one thing can very easily lead to another. I must be honest with you, years ago before I became a Christian, I was guilty of reading some of these books myself. I was probably looking for direction in my life and didn't quite know which way to go. I was looking for some answers, and at that time although I always believed in God, my faith in Him was not great, in fact it was almost non- existent.

So to cut a long story short I ended up looking for answers in the "wrong places," but one thing to bear in mind is that God is a very loving, understanding and forgiving God. Although He sees everything you and I do, if you genuinely don't know any better or don't realise you're doing wrong, God isn't going to strike you down dead or send you to hell just for that, instead He will start to reveal Himself and reveal the Truth to you gradually, bit by bit, piece by piece in a subtle sort of way. God also works through people, for your good, for my good, and for His Divine purposes. People will touch your life and you will touch theirs. For example, have you ever been in a situation where something has been puzzling you or troubling you and you didn't know the answer and then suddenly someone said something in the course of conversation and the "penny dropped?" Some may call it coincidence but it's been my experience that if it's something that is really important for us to know, then God will get the message across to us somehow. But whether we take heed or not is up to us. My personal belief is that God puts the right people in our lives at the right time, in order to direct us and also to fulfil His Divine purposes.

But one thing that always amazes me about horoscopes is how someone could tell you what kind of day you were going to have. For example it might say Monday (Pleasant) Tuesday (Surprising) Wednesday (Sad) Thursday (Disturbing) and so on, all the way throughout the year. This clearly contradicts the Word of God, He tells us *"For this is the day the Lord has made, let us rejoice and be glad in it"* (Ps. 118:24).

Therefore you have the choice to accept what God says or what the horoscope says. Wouldn't you rather "rejoice and be glad every day?" I know this doesn't mean that things are always going to go perfectly for us every day and that we won't have any hurts or problems. Of course we will have problems but, I think God is talking about attitude as well, so that even when things don't go our way, we still have a positive mental attitude towards life.

One person might read a horoscope and simply dismiss it and say what a load of rubbish while another person might read it and believe it wholeheartedly. Remember your subconscious mind creates situations, conditions, and events according to belief. You will attract people, circumstances, or whatever is necessary to make it a reality. The trouble is that most people are unaware of how the mind works and if or when some of these things come true it only serves to convince them that what they read was true. Obviously this is the principle of the self-fulfilling prophecy. Remember that whatever you believe will be true for you, whatever you believe will become your reality.

CHAPTER THREE

Positive Emotions

DESIRE

As Napoleon Hill states in his book, Think and Grow Rich, desire is the starting point for all great achievements. Nothing great in life was ever achieved without first having a burning desire to achieve it. You know when you have a burning desire because it's never far away from your thoughts. Day and night it dominates your thinking and you won't rest until you achieve it.

But obviously to achieve this burning desire, it must be backed up with a plan of action. Just merely wishing or thinking about it isn't going to get you anywhere. The first thing you need to know is exactly what you want to achieve, and it has to be specific and written down. The reason it has to be specific is because your subconscious mind works most effectively when given specific commands. This means that the more specific you are, the better the chance of making it a reality, because the instructions to your subconscious mind will be definite and crystal clear rather than cloudy and vague. For example, if you say, "My goal is to become rich," although that may be your goal, it's too vague and not specific enough. It would be far better to state the actual amount you want to make. For example, you might say, "Five years from now I want to be making an extra million pounds per year," or, "Five years from now I want to own five rental properties," but these are just examples and it is entirely up to you what goals you set. The reason your goals or dreams need to be written down is that it makes it definite to your subconscious mind and gives it something to work on or act upon. Some people might say, "But I know what my goals are. I don't need to write them down." Well that may be better than having no goals at all, but as far as your subconscious mind is concerned, if you haven't written them down, then you haven't set a goal.

Another way to make a powerful impression on your subconscious mind is to have pictures of what you want to achieve and put them in places where you will see them every day. For example, if you want to stay in a bigger house and you want to stay in the countryside rather than in the middle of town and you like the idea of not having any mortgage payments, then you could cut out a picture of the house you want to own and stick it on the refrigerator door with the words "debt free" next to it. The reason I say refrigerator door is that most people use the refrigerator every day.

Remember, out of sight means out of mind; that's why it has to be somewhere you can see it every day. Don't worry about ridicule. Actually, it's to be expected, because all great achievers in life were ridiculed at first, until they became successful. A lot of people will try to discourage you and put you off because they don't want you to get ahead of them. Realise that people who do ridicule you probably do so because they don't have any goals themselves, or they could just be envious of you because you have the guts to step out and do something with your life. Remember, they are not going to pay off your mortgage or provide you with financial security, so why should you listen to them?

Ask yourself, what you would really do with your life if time and money were unlimited? Where would you live? What would you drive? Would you change what you do on a daily basis? What would you do with an extra eight hours a day? Who could you help? The trouble with us is that we think too small and we limit ourselves.

We're not used to dreaming because we've not been taught to dream at school or by our parents. In fact, sometimes we're actually told to behave ourselves or to grow up or that we're living in fantasy land, but I do believe that everybody has some sort of dream. It doesn't necessarily have to be financial; it could be for recognition, it could be to do with athletics, or it could be to give your time or money to a charity or worthy cause. It could be anything, but it's what's important to you that matters. Even though these dreams may have been with us since childhood, they get stuffed so far down inside of us that they're almost unrecognisable and we pretend they're not there.

Teachers, parents, and well meaning but ignorant friends tell us to be "realistic" and ask us what kind of job or career we want to have and immediately limit us to mediocrity. I'm not saying there's anything wrong with jobs or careers, but these people tend not to think outside the box. The trouble is that most of the time we listen to them and accept what they say. Thank goodness the Wright brothers didn't think that way; otherwise, they would never even have attempted to fly in 1903. If Neil Armstrong had been "realistic," do you think he would have attempted to walk on the moon in 1969? Probably not, because people said it couldn't be done. So if you want to be successful in life you're going to have to think differently from the masses. You're going to have to swim upstream and do some things differently than you've been doing up until now.

Dream Big

Many people talk about dreams and many people wish, but very few do anything about it. The Bible tells us, *"The harvest is plentiful but the workers are few,"* (Matthew 9:37).

Less than 5 percent of people ever achieve greatly in life. 95 percent of people work day after day, week after week, year after year for a pay cheque and end up broke after retirement, but you don't have to be one of them. If you work for a boss just now or don't like your job, that's okay because obviously you need money to live and that might be your only source of income. But there's nothing to stop you from starting a part time business of your own that you can work alongside your job to create enough extra income that eventually, if you wish, you can walk away from your day job.

There are many ways to get rich and a lot of millionaires have been created through network marketing businesses. These people were able to keep their full-time jobs, while working their own businesses in their spare time and built it to such a level that they had enough time and money to be able to do what they really wanted with their lives.

As mentioned earlier, dreams and goals are different for everyone, but imagine you didn't have a boss anymore, or if you were making a six-figure income and didn't have to go to work anymore. What would you do with your time? Would you spend more time with your family or would you travel abroad more often? Would you go away for a few months on a cruise instead of just a few weeks at a time? Would the mortgage be taken care of? Would you like to own more than one house? Perhaps own a few rental properties that would bring in enough income to give you financial security? Think of the people in third world countries dying from disease and starvation; how much could you give? How many lives could you save if you were making a six-figure income? The possibilities are almost endless, but it takes money to do these things. Without it our options are limited, but with money we can do a lot of things we would otherwise not have been able to do. How about having a log cabin in the mountains, several thousand feet up, so that you can look down into the valley and see the clouds down below? There's no rush to get back, because you don't need to go to work anymore.

Remember, you are only limited by the size of your thinking, so dream big. God didn't limit us, so why should we limit ourselves? *"No good thing does He withhold from those whose walk is blameless"* (Ps. 84:11), but we've got to get out there and do something. We can't be expecting miraculous results in life if we are not willing to put in the effort. God will help us and direct us, but He's not going to do the work for us.

Desire will give you the motivation and energy to persist in the face of adversity. When your desire is bigger than your fears, nothing will stop you. We must constantly have a dream or desire which we are shooting for, and it must be so big that it outweighs our fears. As soon as we have achieved what we are shooting for, we must have another goal in place, because the worst thing you can do is to achieve a goal then sit back. There's no such thing as standing still; we are either going forward or going backwards.

To the extent you achieve in life will be in direct proportion to the depth of your desire. Remember that nothing is too good to be true and God wants to give you the desires of your heart. *"Delight yourself in the Lord and He will give you the desires of your heart"* (Ps.37:4), but you need to ask Him because He tells us, *"Until now you have not asked for anything in my name, ask and you will receive and your joy will be complete"* (John 16:24).

This does not mean that it's going to be easy. Anything but. But how easy has life been up until now? And how close are you to achieving your dreams? If you keep on doing what you are doing, there is a very high chance that you're going to keep getting what you've always been getting. In other words, if you want a lifestyle you've never had before, you're going to have to do some things you've never done before. You're going to have to step out of your comfort zone and get uncomfortable. You may have to learn new skills. For example, if you're building a network marketing business in your spare time and you currently have a day job working for a boss, then you may have to learn to speak in public, whereas this might never have been previously required working for a boss.

Remember, there's no such thing as something for nothing. There's a price to be paid to be successful in anything, but it's worth it. If success was easy then everybody would be successful and everybody would be wealthy, but not everyone is willing to pay the price. That's why 95 percent of the wealth in the country is owned by only 5 percent of the population. These people are not only willing to pay the price but they also have big dreams— and they know why they are doing something, as opposed to just how to do something. There's a big difference. Sadly 95 percent of the population do not have a reason why; they only know how to do something, and consequently they end up owning just 5 percent of the wealth in the country. But you don't have to be one of them.

Here's How It Works

5% OF THE POPULATION	OWN	95% OF THE WEALTH

(These people are usually self employed or business owners). The 5 per-cent know WHY they are doing something. The 95 percent know HOW to do something.)

95% OF THE POPULATION	OWN	5% OF THE WEALTH

Ninety-five percent of the population usually spends their whole lives working for the 5 percent group, helping them to achieve *their* dreams. Which group would you rather be in? If you said the 5 percent group, that's great— because you'll never be financially free working for a boss. Even if you make really good money, you'll never be free because you'll always have to report back to work; otherwise, you won't get paid. If you want financial freedom, you will need to have a constant stream of income coming in that will continue to keep coming in, regardless of whether you work again or not. This is the difference between ACTIVE INCOME and PASSIVE INCOME, which will be covered later in the book.

The other thing is that there is no longer any such thing as job security. Some people may claim to have a "really good job," but what happens if they get paid off or made redundant? They're in trouble! So don't wait until you're dying of thirst before you dig your well; dig now while the going is good. Think long term and prepare for tomorrow. Who knows, you may be glad you did.

Something for Everyone

On the other hand, there are people who go to work every day who hate their jobs, but they need to go because they need the pay cheque, and that is totally understandable. I can relate because I've been there, but usually this is a sign that there's something better out there for you. You just haven't found it yet. Keep searching. Ask God to help you, and He will. Be patient; keep your eyes and ears open. Look for opportunities, and be open-minded; don't be close minded. Check out everything, but a word of warning: make sure you do check it out. Although there are opportunities out there, there are also a lot of scams out there too, so do your homework and don't just take anybody's advice. Get advice from people who have your interest at heart or who have a vested interest in your success, or you could even get legal advice. But remember that when opportunities do arise, we are not always aware that it is an opportunity at the time.

Thomas Edison said. "Most people miss opportunity because it comes dressed in overalls and looks like work." In other words, it might not come gift wrapped in shiny paper. But I'm firmly convinced that even if you do hate your job, there is something better out there for you. So keep looking and keep searching, but whatever you do, don't sit back and say, "Well, I guess this is it for me, this must be my lot in life." Nothing could be further from the truth. Don't give up.

LOVE

Although this part is entitled Love, it might have been more appropriate to call it Love and Courage. As mentioned earlier, positive and negative emotions cannot co-exist, but it is possible to have more than one positive emotion at the same time or more than one negative emotion at the same time. For example, love and romance could exist simultaneously, as could anger and hatred. But love is the greatest of all the emotions. *"Love is patient, love is kind.*

It does not envy, it does not boast, it is not proud. It is not rude, it is not self-seeking, it is not easily angered, it keeps no record of wrongs. Love does not delight in evil but rejoices with the truth. It always protects always trusts, always hopes, always perseveres" (1 Cor. 13:4-7). When Jesus was asked which was the greatest commandment, He replied; *"Love the Lord your God with all your heart and with all your soul and all your mind. This is the first and greatest commandment. And the second is like it; Love your neighbour as yourself"* (Matt. 22:37-39).

Throughout history many people have given their lives because of love, and although this is necessary sometimes, thankfully we do not have to lay down our lives every time we want to show love to another person. Love can be shown in so many different ways. For example, you show love to your family by the things you do for them. You show love for your husband or wife (or I hope you do) by your deeds or actions and you want to make them happy because you love them. There is love of country; people go to war to fight and die for their country, because they want to defend their homeland and their loved ones. There is love for a fellow human being; for example, there may have been some kind of incident or disaster when you gave your time or money or even risked your life in order to save another human being, even though you might never have met that person in your life. That is true love. *"Greater love has no one than this, that he lay down his life for his friends"* (John 15:13).

Every time I hear that verse I always think of the freedom you and I enjoy today. Our freedom was bought at a price, and we should never forget that. We should never take things for granted. Instead we should have an attitude of gratitude for everything we have. During the Second World War, when democracy itself was at stake, the Nazi war machine hell bent on conquest seemed certain to destroy everything before it. The fate of Great Britain hung in the balance. Hitler had already conquered most of Europe and the odds were stacked massively against us. As soon as France fell in June 1940, Winston Churchill's words were, "The battle for France is over, the Battle of Britain is about to begin." The British knew what was coming next. Hitler wanted to invade Great Britain, but the Germans had to first gain air superiority before they could launch their invasion fleet across the English Channel.

All that stood between the demise of Great Britain and the might of the German Luftwaffe was a few hundred pilots, the Royal Air Force. Some of them were still teenagers, yet they were to change the whole course of the war. The Battle of Britain was a series of dogfights and air raids which started in the summer of 1940 and came to a climax in mid-September. Day by day there were deadly duels in the sky over southeast England, and there were heavy losses on both sides, but even so the R.A.F. could not continue like this because plane for plane we were hopelessly outnumbered. British airfields were constantly targeted and some squadrons had ceased to exist altogether. The pilots, brave as they were, were exhausted. Some of them were flying several sorties a day and sleep became a luxury. The situation was grim and there was a serious shortage of trained pilots. Many had been killed in action and defeat looked inevitable, but they went on, few as they were. For some young, inexperienced pilots taking off, it would be their first and last mission. They probably didn't realise they were heroes at the time. Many had to bail out over the Channel to escape their burning aircraft, having survived combat only to risk drowning or being shot at whilst parachuting.

Then came a miracle. Suddenly the Germans changed tactics. They mistakenly thought that the R.A.F. had been wiped out, and so instead of attacking the airfields, they turned their attention on London and other major cities. This gave the R.A.F. valuable time to repair airfields, to train more pilots, and to regroup. On September 15 the Germans mounted another major daylight attack, expecting no opposition, but this time they were confronted by about three hundred spitfires and hurricanes. On that day fifty-six German planes were shot down, and Hitler called off the invasion of Britain. The Royal Air Force had won the Battle of Britain. Winston Churchill said, "Never in the field of human conflict has so much been owed by so many to so few," and how true that is.

Later on the United States joined us in the war and one American veteran who flew B-17 bombing missions over occupied Europe said that if you were forced to bail out over enemy territory, it was preferable to be captured by the military because sometimes the civilians took the law into their own hands and murdered some of the crewmen when they landed. At the end of the Second World War they revealed the statistics for the number of Allied airmen killed in action over Europe alone.

They were as follows:
Royal Air Force. 55,000 men
U. S. Air Force. 94,000 men

Obviously we owe just as much to servicemen in the Army and Navy, as well as in the Air Force, and when you take into account the losses in the Far East and the Pacific, the figures are astronomical.

Now that may be a strange way to start talking about love, but what greater sacrifice can one make for his fellow countrymen?

Fortunately there are other ways in which we can show love. Sometimes love can be shown just by simply giving someone your time or undivided attention when they are in a time of need. We are all so busy in our daily lives that it is so easy to just say, "I'm sorry, I'm in a real rush just now," or, "I've not got time, can I speak to you later?" and just pass them by. But true love means you treat other people the same way you would like to be treated if you were in their position. In other words, "Do unto others as you would have them do unto you," because who knows when we ourselves might be the person in need?

I can honestly tell you that if it were not for certain people in my life who took the trouble and their valuable time to sit down and talk with me when I was faced with seemingly insurmountable obstacles, you would not be reading this book just now. These people didn't have to sit down and talk with me. They could have decided they were too busy with their own lives to be interested in someone else's problems, but instead they cared and they did what Jesus commanded us to do: *"Love your neighbour as yourself"* (Rom. 13:9).

There are many Bible quotes referring to love, but obviously the greatest example of Love, was Jesus dying on the cross for us. God's love for us is so great that He sent His one and only Son Jesus Christ to be mocked, ridiculed, beaten and eventually crucified so that we might have eternal life in Heaven (see Rom. 5:8). God, our Heavenly Father, wants the best for us, not just eternally but also in our earthly life, so He has to discipline us, just as an earthly father needs to discipline his children. A father or mother disciplines their children, not because they want to, but because of Love. If a child is being rude or defiant or misbehaving in some way, they need to be disciplined. How else are they going to stop doing what they are doing?

This principle is what is known as "tough love." Tough, because it's tough to punish or discipline people we love and its uncomfortable, but long term it will pay dividends. A lot of parents fail to discipline their children because it seems like the easy way out. They say, "Oh anything for an easy life," and just let their children carry on misbehaving. But is it really the easy way out? Yes, you may have avoided an awkward moment of discipline just now, but what about long-term? What about problems that may arise later on in life, such as bad manners, lack of respect, a bad attitude, etc.? Either way you're going to be faced with pain, either the pain of discipline or the pain of regret. The difference is that the pain of discipline lasts a short time, but the pain of regret can last a lifetime.

The Bible gives us clear instruction regarding this subject: *"Do not withhold discipline from a child; if you punish him with the rod, he will not die. Punish him with the rod and save his soul from death"* (Prov. 23:13). Also *"He who spares the rod hates his son, but he who loves him is careful to discipline him,"* (Proverbs 13:24). The trouble is that we think we know best, and when we do that, all we end up with is a whole bunch of problems. Why not trust in God, He won't let you down.

God's Promises for Obedience

Just as God disciplines us when we are heading off track, He also rewards us for obeying Him. He reassures us He is with us always and will never leave us or forsake us (Matt. 28:20 and Josh. 1:5). It is comforting to know that wherever we go and whatever challenges we are faced with, God is with us. This doesn't mean that there won't be any pain or suffering but that we know ultimately everything is in His hands. He tells us: *"If you fully obey the Lord your God and carefully follow all His commands that I give you today, the Lord your God will set you high above all the nations on earth. All these blessings will come upon you and accompany you if you obey the Lord your God. You will be blessed in the city and blessed in the country. The fruit of your womb will be blessed, and the crops of your land and the young of your livestock— the calves of your herds and the lambs of your flocks. Your basket and your kneading trough will be blessed. You will be blessed when you come in and blessed when you go out. The Lord will grant that the enemies who rise up against you will be defeated before you. They will come at you from one direction but flee from you in seven. The Lord will send a blessing on your barns and on everything you put your hand to. The Lord your God will bless you in the land He is giving you. The Lord will establish you as his holy people, as He promised you on oath, if you keep the commands of the Lord your God and walk in His ways. Then all the peoples on earth will see that you are called by the name of the Lord, and they will fear you. The Lord will grant you abundant prosperity— in the fruit of your womb, the young of your livestock and the crops of your ground— in the land he swore to your forefathers to give you. The Lord will open the heavens, the storehouse of his bounty, to send rain on your land in season and to bless all the work of your hands. You will lend to many nations but will borrow from none. The Lord will make you the head, not the tail. If you pay attention to the commands of the Lord your God that I give you this day and carefully follow them, you will always be at the top never at the bottom. Do not turn aside from any of the commands I give you today, to the right or to the left, following other gods and serving them"* (Deut. 28:1-14).

We are also reminded of God's promises for obedience in the book of Leviticus: *"If you follow my decrees and are careful to obey my commands, I will send you rain in its season, and the ground will yield its crops and the trees of the fields their fruit. Your threshing will continue until grape harvest and the grape harvest will continue until planting, and you will eat all the food you want and live in safety in your land. I will grant peace in the land, and you will lie down and no - one will make you afraid. I will remove savage beasts from the land and the sword will not pass through your country.*

You will pursue your enemies, and they will fall by the sword before you. Five of you will chase a hundred, and a hundred of you will chase ten thousand, and your enemies will fall by the sword before you. I will look on you with favour and make you fruitful and increase your numbers, and I will keep my covenant with you. You will still be eating last years harvest when you will have to move it out to make room for the new" (Lev. 26:3-10).

I don't know about you, but I can't think of anything better than being looked upon with favour by the Creator of the universe, can you?

SEX

The emotion of sex is one of the most beautiful emotions a person can experience, but it is also a double-edged sword. If it is used positively it can bring us a lot of happiness and pleasure, but if it is used negatively it can cause us a lot of misery and can even destroy us.

Just as there are positive and negative habits in many other areas in life, so there are positive and negative sexual habits. This is a major area for Satan to play havoc with our minds and bodies and to lure us into addictions and habits that can ruin marriages, relationships, our minds, our happiness, and even our physical bodies. There is a fine line between the positive emotion of sex and the negative emotion of lust, and a lot of people make the mistake of thinking they are one and the same. They are not. They are different, and as a result, a lot of people end up spending a major part of their lives— or in some cases their whole lives— enslaved by a very destructive master. The destructive master can operate in many ways such as fornication, adultery, prostitution, pornography, etc., and you can never be truly happy or successful if something destructive is controlling you. The effects of such destructive habits can be devastating and can result in loneliness, depression, anxiety, disease, and even death. Is it any wonder so many people get addicted to such behaviour when all around us we are being bombarded with sex channels on TV like never before and moral standards are almost non-existent? I'm not saying the TV is totally to blame, but I think it plays a big part. Remember that we all have free will to do whatever we want. God gave us rules and commands to protect us and we have the choice whether to obey or disobey Him. If we obey Him, then our lives will be richly blessed in many ways, but if we disobey Him then we will have to suffer the consequences.

The Wrong Idea of God

I must be completely honest with you. Before I became a Christian I had the wrong idea of God. I thought He was sitting up there in Heaven just waiting to strike us down for the slightest thing we did wrong. I thought that all His commands were designed to make us miserable and unhappy, and whoever passed the misery test got to Heaven. How wrong I was, although at the time I didn't know that. Needless to say, for a large part of my life I cast God aside and decided to do things my way. I thought that my way was the best way, and I was sure it was the best way to happiness and fulfilment. Wrong again— very, very wrong. So I found out the hard way, and my life became one of unhappiness, failure, and frustration, never ever achieving what I wanted. I knew something was missing in my life, but I didn't know what. My life was empty and unfulfilled, and I didn't know why until a few years later

I discovered what was missing. It was Jesus Christ.

Little did I know that the very Person I had cast aside was the answer to every single problem I had. God wants us to bring all our troubles to Him so we don't have to face them alone. God will do things for us that we cannot do for ourselves. We are told in the Bible, *"Then they cried to the Lord in their trouble, and He saved them from their distress. He brought them out of darkness and the deepest gloom and broke away their chains"* (Ps. 107:13-14).

When Jesus tells us, *"I am the way, the truth and the life"* (John 14:6), He means it literally, because if we don't know the way, He is the way; if we don't know the truth, His words are the truth; and if we want a better life, then He is the life and He wants to give us a better life. But the only way for us to get to that better life is to obey Him.

We need to remember that God created marriage to be good and He also created sex to be good, but to be enjoyed only within marriage. I know this will be a major stumbling block for some people, but remember that the toughest decisions bring the biggest rewards and God never closes one door without opening another. It has been my experience that every time God has opened a new door for me, it has always been far greater than the door to which I was accustomed. The trouble is that we get into a rut sometimes and we don't believe there is a better way. In fact, usually we don't even take time out to try and think if there is a better way. A lot of people will criticise or ridicule God's "door," but how can you ridicule something you've never been through? Why not go through it and if you don't like it you can always go back to your own "door?"

God also wants to protect you from unwanted pregnancies, maintenance payments, disease, and possible death because He cares for you (1 Peter 5:7). Some people may scoff at this and say, "Isn't that a bit old fashioned? Don't you think you should change with the times?" Well, some things may change with the times, such as fashion and technology, etc., but God's word is one thing that never changes, ever! "Heaven and earth will pass away but my words will never pass away" (Matt. 24:35).

Illusions

The dictionary defines the word illusion as a "deceptive appearance or belief," and that is precisely how the devil works. The devil is constantly trying to lead us astray by messing up our minds and our belief systems by convincing us that his way is going to give us more happiness and pleasure. One of the ways the devil does this is through pornography. The reason pornography is an illusion is because it is a trap.

It may look tempting and inviting initially, but the reality is one of unhappiness and loneliness. Do you think God wants you to be unhappy and lonely? Of course not. He wants the best for you. That's why He tells us, "But seek first His Kingdom and His righteousness and all these things will be given to you as well" (Matt. 6:33), and that includes relationships!

One of the best quotes I ever read on this subject was by Edwin Louis Cole, author of Communication Sex and Money, and he said, "Pornography promises to serve and please, but only enslaves and dominates." I think that is an excellent way of putting it. He also mentions that one psychologist reckoned it could take four to five years of therapy to rid patients of sexual addictions; therefore, it's also going to take us a bit of time. We also need to remember the danger of negative emotions created by pornography. Remember that whatever you give away you receive, and whatever you lust after you lack. That applies to anything, not just money.

What does God have to say about such behaviour? Well, He makes it perfectly clear in the book of Matthew: *"Woe to the world because of the things that cause people to sin! Such things must come, but woe to the man through whom they come! If your hand or your foot causes you to sin, cut it off and throw it away. It is better for you to enter life maimed or crippled than to have two hands or two feet and be thrown into eternal fire. And if your eye causes you to sin gouge it out and throw it away. It is better for you to enter life with one eye than to have two eyes and be thrown into the fire of hell"* (Matt. 18:7-9)

Temptation

Everyone has to deal with temptation some time in their lives. It's not a question of *if* we are tempted; it's a case of ***when*** we are tempted. The important thing is how we respond. As Edwin Louis Cole explains in his book, the emotion of sex is perfectly normal and natural and cannot and should not be suppressed. But sometimes we find ourselves in situations when our emotions threaten to overwhelm us, to the extent that we disregard what's right and what's wrong. Some people risk their marriages, careers, friendships, and reputations when they give in to their emotions, and sometimes the consequences can last a lifetime.

Although the emotion of sex is a very strong and powerful emotion, we need to remember our conscious minds make the decisions. We all must take responsibility for our actions, because ultimately we will be held responsible. The Bible tells us, "Like a city whose walls are broken down is a man who lacks self-control," (Prov. 25:28). Not only do we leave ourselves wide open to a variety of troubles, but this can lead to further negative emotions. Emotions such as guilt, fear, anxiety, worry, and even depression can result from unlawful sexual relations and can plague us both physically and mentally. How can we ever hope to be truly happy and successful when dealing with such emotions?

Some people might be fooled into thinking that because no one else knows about the affair they are having, they're off the hook and everything will be just fine. Well, they're forgetting that the two most important people know, and that is God and their own subconscious mind. You cannot escape your own mind, and you cannot escape God's judgment, so it really makes little difference if no one else knows. God has commanded us not to commit adultery and not to covet our neighbour's wife or anything belonging to our neighbour, (Exodus 20:14-17), but He has also promised us that when we are tempted, He will help us by providing us with a way out and He won't let us be tempted beyond what we can bear (1 Cor. 10:13). This doesn't mean it will be easy to do but life wasn't meant to be easy, and remember, life is a test. Each time you are tempted to do something wrong and you resist it, your self-confidence grows and your self-image improves, which in turn gives you more strength to resist future temptations. So once again it's going to be an upward spiral or a downward spiral, depending on your response.

I believe there is also a connection between prosperity and doing what's right in the eyes of God. We are told, *"Misfortune pursues the sinner, but prosperity is the reward of the righteous"* (Prov. 13:21), but at the same time we must remember that a fresh start is always possible with God and His love for us is so great that no matter what we've done wrong or how badly we've messed up, God is always willing to forgive us and give us another chance. He tells us, *"and when you and your children return to the Lord your God and obey Him with all your heart and with all your soul according to everything I command you today, then the Lord your God will restore your fortunes and have compassion on you and gather you again from all the nations where He scattered you. Even if you have been banished to the most distant land under the heavens, from there the Lord your God will gather you and bring you back. He will bring you to the land that belonged to your fathers and you will take possession of it. He will make you more prosperous and numerous than your fathers"* (Deut. 30:2-5).

ROMANCE

Romance is the emotion that adds sparkle to a relationship and keeps it alive. Some people make the mistake of thinking that because they've been in a relationship for a long time and they've met their ideal partner, being romantic doesn't matter anymore. They may have been romantic in the early stages of the relationship, but now that they feel they've achieved their goal, so to speak, they stop working at it and take their partner for granted. But remember, nothing in life is guaranteed— including relationships. When you take romance out of a relationship, it can quite easily stagnate or go stale. You've got to be working as hard to stay there as you did to get there. It's easy to get into a rut or a situation where week after week, month after month, year after year, nothing changes; it's just the same old routine. For example, some people no longer buy their partner Valentine's cards or Christmas cards or tell them they love them. Other things that may have fallen by the wayside might include going out together for a meal or going to the cinema, holding hands when walking along the road, offering to help with some household chores, buying unexpected gifts, or simply opening a door for them. You may be tempted to think that some of these things are small and unimportant, but sometimes it can be the little difference that makes the big difference.

If going out dating together at the beginning of the relationship was fun and exciting, why shouldn't it still be fun now? And why should it stop? Why not schedule a certain amount of time every week when you and your partner can spend some quality time together and do something romantic so that you can give each other your undivided attention? Allocate yourselves a certain amount of time every week and stick to it. No matter how busy you are or how hectic a week it has been, make it a priority to have a certain amount of time together on a regular basis. Some people may claim that their lives are too busy to take time out to be romantic, but that's exactly the reason you need to do it. How important is your relationship to you?

The busier your schedule is, the more important it is to have this quality time. Remember that if your partner's needs are not being met, they may seek what they're looking for elsewhere. Not that I'm saying they should or they shouldn't, but it's a fact of life.

Different Wiring

It has been proven that women's brains are wired differently from men's brains. Generally speaking, before a woman's sexual needs are met, her emotional needs must first be met; whereas a man's needs are mainly physical and a much higher percentage of men would be willing to have a sexual encounter regardless if their emotional needs had been met or not. Women also have the advantage of being more perceptive than men when it comes to reading body language. When two people are talking to each other, most of the communication which takes place is unspoken. Allan Pease explains in his book Body Language that 55 percent of the message is conveyed through body language; this means signals and gestures which happen subconsciously and most of the time we are not even aware of it. 38% of the message is conveyed by the tone of voice, and only 7 percent of the message is conveyed by the actual words spoken.

Have you ever heard the saying "It's not what you say it's how you say it?" There is a lot of truth in that, especially if you have to tell somebody something that could possibly offend them. For example, suppose you have to give someone some constructive criticism in order to help them, but the actual words are going to be quite harsh. If you speak in a very polite and tactful manner, use a friendly tone of voice, and say it with a smile, you will probably get away with it without causing too much offense. But on the other hand, if you say something very abruptly and with a scowl on your face, it won't really matter what the actual words are, the message received will not be a friendly one.

The one thing we cannot hide is our body language. It gives us away every time. Women are more likely to know what's on a man's mind than the other way about. God has obviously seen fit to endow women with the advantage in this particular area, probably quite appropriately given the nature of the male species.

Relationships

Many problems arise in relationships because of a lack of communication. When people don't communicate they don't find out the facts and when they don't find out the facts they assume. And when they assume, they're usually wrong and they make faulty assumptions, and when they do that they're never going to solve the problem.

There's nothing worse than a problem in a relationship that isn't discussed. It festers away and eats away at the people involved and can ruin the relationship. No matter how damaging or hurtful the facts are or how much we don't want to hear them, it's always far better to know the facts, because at least that way we know where we stand and from there we can work through it or move on.

No problem will ever be solved without talking about it. Also, a lot of people play the "if only" game. They may be in a relationship and say, "Things would be just great if only my partner didn't have these relatives," or, "If only my partner didn't do this or didn't do that," but we need to realise that some things can be changed and some things can't. Whatever it is that we're not happy about, the first thing we need to ask ourselves is, "Can this be changed or not?"

If it is something which can be changed, at least there is hope. There is a possibility an improvement can be made in that area. For example; if your partner had a negative attitude, by changing what goes into their mind they could start to develop a more positive attitude. But some things simply cannot be changed. For example, your partner may have children from a previous marriage with whom you don't get along. In that case you have to realise it's a package deal.

There's no point saying "if only" they didn't have these children because they do. Saying "if only" or wishing isn't going to change anything, so you either have to accept the whole situation or move on. Some people play the "if only" game for years and they burn themselves out mentally in the process.

THINGS THAT CAN'T BE CHANGED	THINGS THAT CAN BE CHANGED
My partner has a child from a previous marriage.	My partner lives far away.
Mt partner is only five feet tall.	My partner is selfish.
My partner has relatives that I don't like.	My partner leaves a mess wherever she goes.
My partner has to keep in contact with her ex spouse for the sake of the children.	My partner has a negative attitude or habit.

Realise that situations, or life itself, is never going to be perfect. If it wasn't that particular problem then it would be some other problem. I've never met anyone yet who has the perfect situation or relationship.

FAITH

Faith is a very powerful emotion and can literally work miracles in your life. Faith is believing what is unseen just now will eventually become your reality. Faith is believing, with God's help, all obstacles can be overcome, no matter how big they are. In the book of Matthew we are told, *"If you have faith as small as a mustard seed, you can say to this mountain, move from here to there and it will move. Nothing will be impossible for you"* (Matt. 17:20).

No problem is too big for God. Although circumstances and problems may threaten to overwhelm us at times, we must remember that God is watching over us and He is in overall command. It's not the government, it's not the politicians or the military, but God. As we are told about the mustard seed, you don't have to have a lot of faith— although it's better if you do— but you only need to have just enough to tip the scales in a positive direction. Jesus tells us not to doubt but to believe and have faith and we will receive whatever we ask for in prayer (Matt. 21:21-22).

There are many enemies of faith, such as fear, worry, and doubt, and it is impossible to have faith while these emotions are occupying your mind. It's almost as if faith and fear are opposite ends of the same stick. But if you don't have much faith just now, that's okay; just go with what you have, and as you start to trust in God, your faith will gradually start to strengthen. Someone once said that faith is like a muscle, it can be developed over time. I have found this to be very true.

When I first became a Christian my faith was probably as small as a mustard seed, maybe even smaller. But each time God did something for me, my faith grew a little bit and I started to trust in Him more and more. This doesn't mean we will automatically get everything we ask for, because it depends what it is we are asking for. If it's something which isn't going to be beneficial for us, God isn't going to give us anything that may harm us. The trouble is, sometimes we are convinced that what we ask for is going to be good for us, but that is not always the case. Imagine a four-year-old child asking their mother or father if they can play with a box of matches; what do you think their response would be? Well, if they are responsible, loving parents who want the best for their child, the answer would be no because of the dangers involved. But the child can't see the dangers and doesn't understand why Mum and Dad won't give them the matches, so they get upset and they think Mum and Dad are just simply being rotten.

Although the parents can clearly see the dangers, the child cannot. We need to understand that sometimes we don't always get what we ask for because we can't see the dangers, but our Father in Heaven who knows everything and sees everything cares for us. I do believe God works in mysterious ways and sometimes we don't always get what we ask for because He has something better for us instead. But once again, we are not usually aware of this and can quickly become despondent or cynical when we don't get what we think we want.

If we want miracles to take place in our lives, then the faith must come before the results, not after. You cannot be saying, "Well, I'll wait and see if it happens, and then I'll have faith," because it will probably never happen. When two blind men approached Jesus and asked to be healed, Jesus said to them, "Do you believe that I am able to do this?" "Yes, Lord," they replied. Then He touched their eyes and said, *"According to your faith will it be done to you,"* and their sight was restored (Matt. 9:29-30).

Notice how the blind men had to have the faith first, before they were healed. But faith is not always connected to religion. For example, if you work for a boss or have your own business, you have faith you're going to get paid for the work you've done. Usually you do the work first and then get paid, but suppose you had no faith at all? You wouldn't even get out of your bed in the morning, because what would be the point?

If you plant some seeds in the garden, you have faith they're going to grow, otherwise you wouldn't bother. All the time we are operating in the realms of faith, probably without us even realising it or thinking about it.

If you are starting out in a business of your own, just the fact that you have started, proves you have some amount of faith; otherwise you would never have taken that step. But remember, faith has no logic to it. It is not our job to figure out the "how to" or "how" this will be possible. It is only our job to believe and to have faith. Leave the "how to" to a Power greater than yourself to figure out. Some people may refer to this power as God, others may refer to it as the subconscious mind, but whatever you believe, remember that a journey of a thousand miles begins with a single step and if we are too concerned about the journey ahead of us then we might trip over the step right in front of us. If you were going to climb a mountain and you were standing at the bottom, although you had faith that you would get to the top, there's no way you could guarantee exactly how things would work out all the way to the top and back. It's the same in business and in life.

All the time things are changing as we progress on our journey and we may have to adapt or change our strategy along the way. Of course we still need to plan our journey, but we should have no anxiety about it, nor will we always understand why certain things happen. *"A man's steps are directed by the Lord. How then can anyone understand his own way?"* (Prov. 20:24).

Sometimes in life things happen which some people may call coincidence, and I admit that certain things cannot be proven. At the same time, we are all entitled to our own beliefs. I remember a few years ago when I was faced with seemingly insurmountable obstacles and one particular problem had been weighing on my mind for some time. I asked God to help me because I didn't know what to do. In fact I asked Him a few times, but there didn't seem to be any reply forthcoming and I thought He had forgotten about me. Then one day when I was driving on the other side of town, I was driving past a church but it wasn't my local church. It was Sunday evening and the street outside was quite busy because a lot of people were making their way into the church for the evening service. They all looked so cheerful and happy as they greeted each other, and I thought to myself, wouldn't it be great to be as happy as that? And consequently I felt a strange urge to go in. In fact the urge was so strong I knew if I didn't go in I would feel really bad. So I thought, Why not? So I went in and sat down, and to my utter amazement the thing the minister was talking about was exactly the same thing I had been asking God. This lead to my question being answered and a weight being lifted off my shoulders. Needless to say, I came out of there a whole lot happier than when I went in. Someone once said that coincidence is when God chooses to remain anonymous.

If we cast our minds back to 7 December 1941, the Japanese had just delivered a devastating blow to the United States Pacific Fleet. The Japanese aim was to launch a surprise attack on Pearl Harbour and totally destroy everything in it, so America would have no means of retaliating. On that day many different warships were at Pearl Harbour— except for the aircraft carriers.

The American carriers were at sea and they escaped destruction that day. Ironically, six months later during the Battle of Midway, the Japanese suffered heavy losses when they lost four aircraft carriers after being attacked by U.S. aircraft.

The planes that sunk the Japanese carriers were planes from the U.S. carriers which had escaped destruction at Pearl Harbour six months earlier. Was it just coincidence that the American carriers were at sea that day or was it Divine intervention? No one can say for sure, but even the Bible recognises that there are times when war is necessary (Deut. 20), and God also makes it clear that He plays a part in the final outcome: *The horse is made ready for the day of battle, but victory rests with the Lord"* (Prov. 21:31).

The reason I include these examples is that we may be tempted at times to think God has abandoned us, but He is still with us.

Footprints

One night I had a dream.

I dreamed I was walking along

the beach with God, and across

the sky flashed scenes

from my life. For each scene I

noticed two sets of footprints in the sand.

One belonged to me and the other to God

When the last scene of my life flashed before

us I looked back at the footprints in the sand.

I noticed that at times along the path of life

there was only one set of footprints. I also

noticed that it happened at the very lowest

and saddest times of my life. This really

bothered me and I questioned God about it.

"God, you said that once I decided to follow

you, you would walk with me all the way, but I

noticed that during the most troublesome

times in my life there is only one set

of footprints. I don't understand why, in

times when I needed you most, you would

leave me." God replied, "My precious,

precious child, I love you and I would never,

never leave you during your times of trials

and suffering. When you see only one set of

footprints, it was then that I carried you."

— Margaret Fishback Powers

HOPE

Hope is very similar to the emotion of faith; in fact, some people call this emotion "baby faith." Hope is not quite as powerful as faith, although it is a very important emotion to have. The difference is that faith goes a stage further because it actually believes whatever it is you have faith in will actually become your reality. Hope doesn't necessarily believe it will happen, although it does hope, and there's nothing wrong with living in hope. For example, if someone buys lottery tickets, they obviously hope they are going to win but they may not believe they are going to win. I'm not advocating gambling, but that is just an example.

It doesn't matter what our plans are or what situation we are in, we must never give up hope. Without hope, what else is there? Someone once said, "there are no hopeless situations, only people without hope." That's easy to say when everything is going well, but what happens when the chips are down? Will we still have hope then? I'd like to think so because to give up hope is to become hopeless. Although sometimes in life we may be defeated, we should not give up hope, because there is always something to be learned from defeat. Henry Ford said "Failure is just an opportunity to begin again more intelligently."

What is the alternative to the positive emotion of hope? Obviously when you take away the positive, it is immediately replaced by the negative, which in this case would be despair. It is a sad fact today that a lot of people commit suicide. People, through no fault of their own, have been driven to despair for whatever reasons and feel that they can't handle life anymore. I honestly believe a lot of these people don't really want to die, but they can see no way out of the situation they are in and they have given up hope. I also believe a lot of suicides could be prevented if these people believed there was a way out of their problems and if there was even the slightest glimmer of hope.

It's up to you and I to share with people that there is a better way to think and there is a better way to live and there is hope for the future. We also have a Father in heaven who cares for us. Hope and despair are opposite ends of the same stick, just as fear, doubt, and worry are at the opposite end of the stick of faith. If we were to sketch these diagrams out, they would look like this:

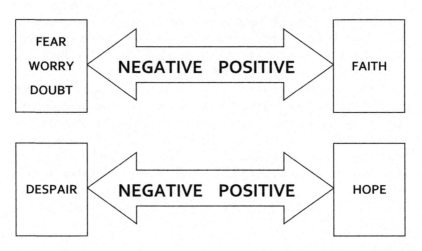

When it comes to emotions, there is no in-between. You're either operating with a positive or a negative mindset. Why add to your troubles by entertaining more negative emotions than you have to? The book of Proverbs tell us, "Hope deferred makes the heart sick, but a longing fulfilled is a tree of life" (Prov. 13:12). Once again the Bible is reminding us of the effects of emotions on our physical health. If a person has hope when others all around him have given up hope, he is to be commended for it, for he is a positive thinker. Too many times we hear people say, "Don't get your hopes up." For example, someone may have been presented with an opportunity of some kind and their friends or parents say, "Don't get your hopes up and that way you won't be disappointed." What a negative statement if I ever heard one. Obviously these people mean well, but if you really think about it, if they're saying, "Don't get your hopes up," what are they offering you or suggesting instead?

There is only one alternative to hope and that is hopelessness, because if you don't have hope, then why even bother to start? There would be no point. The person operating without hope is a sad individual, but at the same time I believe that most people do have some kind of hope, otherwise how would they make it through the day? Some people may say, "But what if you get your hopes up and things don't work out for you? Obviously you'll be even more disappointed." Well, that may be true, but you've just got to be able to handle it. That may sound a bit harsh, but if you want to be successful at anything, you've got to be able to handle disappointment now and again.

If you can't handle disappointment then you probably won't get very far, because the truth is, the more successful a person is, the more disappointment they've had to endure and the more obstacles they've had to overcome to get there. There's no such thing as a smooth, painless, hassle-free road to success.

When you are faced with disappointment, your response is everything. This is where the rubber meets the road. This is what separates the winners from the losers. You can either quit or go on. The winners will go on regardless of how tough it gets. If you persist in spite of your disappointments, your ability to handle future disappointments increases and you become stronger mentally and emotionally.

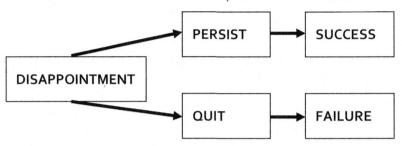

Which road will you take? Only you can decide. It is impossible to persist and not have hope because your very actions prove that you do. When you have hope, you will be acting as though you are going to succeed instead of expecting to fail, and there's a world of difference. Remember, expectation is a powerful force constantly attracting things to us. So hope for the best, expect the best, and get the best.

Another negative saying we sometimes hear is; "Sounds too good to be true." Usually we hear this when we present someone with a fabulous idea with the potential for making a lot of extra money. Isn't it strange how no one ever doubts anything bad, but when it's something exceptionally good they tend to doubt it? I guess it's a case of once bitten twice shy. I'm sure we've all been "bitten" or "stung" more than once in our lives, and it makes us sceptical. But it's good to be sceptical; they say being sceptical is a sign of a good business person. It only becomes a handicap when we become either cynical or close-minded. Those are not good traits to have if you want to be successful because a close-minded person will miss every opportunity.

Realise, nothing is too good to be true. There are countless examples of people who started with virtually nothing and made their dreams come true, people who went from rags to riches because they had a dream and they had hope. They maybe started off the same way and thought, "Sounds too good to be true," but they had a little bit of hope and decided to step out on faith. So if they can do it, why can't you? The only thing that will keep you from your dreams is you, so don't give up. Keep going and think of hope as being like a flame. Sometimes it burns brighter than at other times. Sometimes it might flicker and look a bit shaky, but even when it's shaky, it can always be rekindled and brought back to life. As long as it never goes out it doesn't matter how shaky it gets, just keep the flame alive.

ENTHUSIASM

Enthusiasm can literally spell the difference between success and failure in anything you do. You might have the greatest idea or plan in the world, but if you're not enthusiastic about it then why should anybody else be? Enthusiasm is a very positive emotion that radiates from you, and people can tell if you are enthusiastic or not because it leaks out in your body language. Things such as your posture, tone of voice, the look in your eyes, and your facial expression are constantly expressing your inward emotions. If you are sharing an idea with someone and you avoid making eye contact, they won't trust you and they won't believe you. They'll think to themselves, "What's he hiding? He won't look me in the eye." It's almost as if people can tell what's going on in your mind by the look in your eyes, so it's important to make eye contact.

Enthusiasm is contagious, and people will either be attracted to you or repelled by you depending on whether you are enthusiastic or not. Think about it: who are you more attracted to? A person who is full of fun and enthusiasm or a person with a negative outlook who is always complaining?

Nobody wants to be around a whiner, which is probably the opposite of enthusiasm, but if you are enthusiastic, people will be attracted to you like bees round honey. People will want to be around you just to see what's going on. I've known people who were independent business owners and people would join them in the business just because they were enthusiastic. People knew that if they were that enthusiastic about it, then it must be a good idea, and they didn't want to get left behind.

When I think of enthusiasm, I am reminded of a lady called Jane. Jane had many friends, and people loved to be around her because of her positive attitude. She had a lot of enthusiasm for her work and whatever tasks she was asked to do. While some people would complain about their work, she never complained but happily did whatever she had to do. She always had a smile on her face, and if you asked her how she was she would reply, "Great! How are you?" Jane could literally change the atmosphere in a room, just by walking in. Her enthusiasm was contagious, and you could gradually notice the change in the atmosphere as she spoke and laughed with people. She was a pleasure to be around and took a sincere interest in other people and their problems. She didn't wait for people to take an interest in her but rather took an interest in them. She was always looking to help people out and would always go the extra mile. Instead of doing just enough, she would do a little bit more, expecting nothing in return. She seldom took the credit, but instead she would give the credit to other people, and as a result of her positive attitude she got promoted. Notice how the attitude came before the promotion. A lot of people have their thinking back to front. They may say, "Once I get promoted or once I get a raise, then I'll be more enthusiastic," but it doesn't work that way. The enthusiasm and the positive attitude must come first. Whether you're a business owner or an employee or whatever it is you plan to do, if you want positive results then the attitude must come first. Wouldn't it be great to have more people like Jane in the workplace? Are there any Jane's at your workplace? If not, why not become one yourself (obviously use your own name) and, who knows, you may be the one who inspires other people. We cannot change the world directly, but we can influence it by changing ourselves. As Norman Vincent Peale said "Enthusiasm makes the difference."

We also need to remember that "How are you?" is a question we are all asked very frequently, so it's important that we answer positively. Instead of just saying, "Allright" or "Not bad" which are average answers at best, we need to say, "Great" or something similar, such as, "Good" or "Fantastic" or "Tremendous," because remember, what you say is what you get. You don't wait until you're feeling great, before you say "Great." because it may never happen. You speak the words first (which are affirmations), and this will start to change your attitude. If you say, "Not bad," then you are programming yourself just to be "not bad."

Like any positive emotion, enthusiasm can be quickly killed off by the presence of any negative emotions. Enthusiasm has to be protected and constantly reinforced by maintaining a positive attitude and by controlling what goes into your mind. Enthusiasm is quite a fragile emotion, easily shattered or lost depending on your response to particular events or situations. It's a fight to stay positive, and we have to work at it continuously. No positive attitude will long endure without constant daily reinforcement. It's easy to be negative and we do not have to try to be negative; it will happen automatically if we do not control our attitude and what we allow into our minds.

It's a mental battle that takes place daily and never stops. We never get to a point where we no longer require positive input, because no matter what we are enthusiastic about, whether its keeping fit or some kind of project or expanding a business, somewhere along the line we are going to be faced with disappointment, chal-lenges, setbacks, fear, and discouragement— and what will happen to our enthusiasm then? Will we still be as enthusiastic as we were at the beginning? Probably not, and this is where the majority of people quit. It's a sad fact of life that the majority of people quit the majori-ty of things they undertake. At some point along the line their enthusiasm starts to fade until eventually they give up. So we need to be reading positive books and listening to motivational CDs on a regular basis.

We also need to associate on a regular basis with people who are more successful than we are and who have already succeeded at what we are trying to do. This will keep you enthusiastic, in spite of all the adversity and challenges that are bound to come your way. Winners also do what they need to do, even when they don't feel like doing it. But if you don't feel enthusiastic, how do you be-come enthusiastic? You do it by forcing yourself to do something, even when you don't want to do it, and as you do this, you will start to become enthusiastic.

It's a psychological principle that motion creates emotion. You also need to avoid negative sources of input such as newspa-pers, TV, and negative people, as this will kill your enthusiasm faster than anything. How often do you pick up a newspaper or watch the news on TV and come away feeling extremely motivated or excited about what's going on in the world? How do you feel after talking about your dreams and ambitions with someone who is negative and tells you that it won't work? Excited? Enthu-siastic? Probably not. So it's up to you and it's a conscious choice, so make it a positive choice.

Enthusiasm is also closely related to the emotion of humour. If you have humour, it shows you are enthusiastic. It makes all the difference and is actually good for your health, both physiolog-ically and mentally. The Bible once again reminds us of the connection between what goes on in our minds and our physical bodies: *"A cheerful heart is good medicine; but a crushed spirit dries up the bones"* (Prov. 17:22).

CHAPTER FOUR

Stress

Stress is something which affects all of us at some time or another. People can easily feel "stressed out," depending on what's happening in their lives. But what actually is stress? Stress is a state of mind. When situations threaten to overwhelm us or we are faced with several problems or tasks to deal with all at the same time, we can feel stressed. This is because our conscious minds can only deal with one thing at a time and our conscious minds can only think one thought at a time. If you are dealing with one problem while mentally trying to deal with other problems at the same time, you will feel stressed. The more things that are weighing on your mind and the more things you have to remember, the more stressed you will be. This is because each thing takes up a certain amount of mental energy.

A great way to combat this is by using a notebook or diary. Using a notebook won't necessarily solve your problems, but at least you won't be wasting mental energy by trying to remember things. I personally couldn't get by without using a notebook because there would simply be far too much to remember. It is far simpler just to write everything down, and that way you won't have to worry about forgetting anything either. It also frees up your mind for other more important tasks and allows you to think more creatively. Instead of trying to remember different things, you only have to remember to look at your notebook. This not only reduces stress but also increases your effectiveness and productivity. As you accomplish each task it's a good idea to score it off. By doing this, you can actually see yourself making progress. You may not always accomplish everything on the list, but at least you are working towards it and you are clear in your own mind about what's been done and what's still to be done. This alone will make you feel better about yourself.

Suppose you had ten things on your list to be accomplished today. The first thing you need to do is prioritise your list, and decide what things you are going to do first. As you work through your list you want to give 100 percent of your attention to the present task only, and as you move on to the next task, forget about the previous task and give 100 percent of your focus and energy to this particular task. Don't worry about the next task or the previous task, but learn to live mentally in the present moment, which is all you can do. You will find that as you do this, you will be operating with maximum effectiveness. As you start to make this new way of thinking a habit, you will find that you have more peace of mind, a lower stress level, and are more relaxed. Some people burn themselves out by mentally trying to live in the past or the future, and as a result they are less effective in the present moment. You cannot live in the past or the future, not even for a split second, so why even waste energy trying?

It really comes down to mental attitude. It's not so much the circumstances themselves but rather how you look at them. Attitude is everything— in fact, it is one thing over which you have absolute control. There is no stress in a situation itself. Stress only exists in our heads, and anything that's in our heads can be controlled.

Stress is a state of mind created by our response to particular events or situations. Notice how the stress is created by our response (something within our control) and not by the events or situations themselves (things we cannot control). If you slept in one morning and as soon as you opened your eyes you saw it was 8:55 A.M. and you were due to be at the office at 9:00 A.M. and you still had to get ready and it was an hour's drive to get there, what would your response be? Obviously you are going to be late, but whether you got stressed or not would depend on your response. You could either be relaxed and late or stressed and late, but either way you are going to be late.

If you immediately jumped out of bed, pulled on the nearest set of clothes, didn't even bother to have breakfast or look in the mirror, ran about like crazy trying to gather your stuff for work, and ran out the door within ten minutes of opening your eyes, then you are going to be stressed. But on the other hand you could choose, if you wish, to lie in bed for an extra five minutes before getting up. You could think to yourself, "Well, I'm late anyway and I'm not going to be stressed out but I'm going to lie here for five more minutes and plan what I'm going to do. I may not have time to cook anything for breakfast or have a cup of tea, but I've got some sandwiches in the fridge which I'll take with me while I'm travelling to work and that'll save a bit of time. Also, the paperwork I was going to do this morning at home, I can catch up with later because it's not urgent. And I'll take my mobile phone with me, so that way I can phone in to work at some point on the way there. And I've just remembered I've got a brand new suit I can wear to save me looking for my other one and that'll save me a bit more time." Now that is just an example, but you can see how the different responses would cause completely different levels of stress?

Relaxation is the key to eliminating stress, and this in turn helps us to think more clearly. It has also been proven that it is impossible to feel fear or anxiety when your muscles are totally relaxed. Humour is also a good antidote for stress. Have you ever had a really good laugh and felt stressed out at the same time? Probably not, because it's impossible. If we are feeling stressed out we should take time out to recall some funny moments and have a good laugh, or you could even watch one of your favourite comedies. Remember, laughter is one of the best medicines there is, and it costs nothing. I think we are all guilty of taking ourselves too seriously at times. Life is too short to be too serious all the time. Practice laughing more and smiling more.

We all smile and laugh when we are happy, but do you realise this process also works in reverse? For example, if you are not happy but force yourself to smile, you will feel happier. This is because the muscles in our body are linked to our brain, and when we force ourselves to smile, the brain picks this up and this in turn affects our thoughts and we think positive thoughts. Your posture also affects how you feel about yourself. Do you stand up straight or do you slouch? Are your muscles tensed or relaxed? Even when you are on the phone to someone, people can tell your state of mind without even being able to see you. The state of mind you have will come across to them. Obviously your tone of voice plays a part, but there's more to it than that. It's like a sixth sense or a gut feeling people get. It's as if your subconscious is communicating with their subconscious. So you want to stack everything in your favour and make sure your state of mind is positive. The next time you are on the phone to someone, stand up straight with your chin up and your shoulders back and a smile on your face, then notice how much more positive you feel. Also practice talking faster as this also helps you to feel more enthusiastic, which will also come across.

Relaxation

Sometimes during the course of a day, it is a good idea just to take a few minutes now and again to simply relax or switch off. It doesn't have to be for long; just five minutes of relaxation during the course of a busy day can make all the difference. Simply sitting still with your eyes shut and relaxing your body will help to rid the body of stress and will increase your energy. Try to be as still and as relaxed as possible. Make sure you are not thinking about work or problems or anything that will cause stress. Try to blank all these things out, just for five minutes. If you must think of something, make sure it is something peaceful or tranquil— for example, being on a tropical beach or out in the countryside where it is nice and peaceful and the only sounds to be heard are the wildlife and running water from a nearby river. Imagine how peaceful it would be without any traffic or noise you would normally experience in town.

You can think about whatever you want to but the main point of the exercise is just to relax. It's important to keep your eyes shut during these brief few minutes because 25 percent of all our energy is used up through the eyes. Not only that, but if your eyes are open then you will find yourself getting distracted or thinking about other things.

Some people may say, "I've not got time to do that, I'm too busy." Well, they've missed the point because that is exactly why they need to do it. Everybody can find five minutes during the course of a day, it doesn't matter how busy you are.

It reminds me of the story of the lumberjack who was going to chop down a tree with an axe. The problem was that his axe was blunt and he only had twenty minutes to chop it down. So instead of slogging away at the tree for twenty minutes with a blunt axe, he decided to take five minutes out to sharpen the axe. This left him fifteen minutes to chop down the tree, but because his axe had been sharpened and was much more effective, he was able to successfully chop down the tree in the allotted time. The moral of the story is that it is much better to have a highly effective fifteen minutes than to have an unproductive twenty minutes. You could look upon your time of relaxation as sharpening your axe. You may think you have lost five minutes, but it will help you be more productive during the rest of the day.

Attitude

It has been said that our attitude is our most priceless possession, and I totally agree with that because it colours and taints
everything we look at. In fact, our attitude will determine how successful we become in life. Our attitude also determines how happy
we are and it affects our level of stress. You could compare attitude
to looking through a pair of tinted glasses. Imagine looking through
glasses with a red tint in them. No matter what you look at, whether
it's good or bad, pleasant or ugly, everything will be tinted red. Now
imagine that the tint itself is the attitude. In this case, imagine the red
tint is a positive attitude. It doesn't matter what you are looking at,
you will find the good in every person and every situation. You can't
help but see it, because that's your attitude. But imagine looking
through glasses with a blue tint in them, what will you see then? Obviously everything will be coloured blue. Now imagine that the
blue tint is a negative attitude. It wouldn't matter if you were
looking at the most beautiful sight in the world, you would tend to
find fault with everything or everyone because that would also be
your attitude. My question to you is, what's your tint? Is it red or is it
blue? If it's blue, then it's never too late to change. You can have a
red tint anytime you choose, because it is a choice. Attitude is
always a choice. Some people blame what they see or even blame
the glasses but never ever question the tint itself. If we want our
world to change then we must take responsibility for our attitude
and we must change ourselves.

Sometimes in life we are faced with many problems all at the
same time and we can easily feel stressed. This is because we
are only human and we can only deal with one thing at a time, so
we are bound to feel a certain amount of stress. Before we decide
which problem we are going to deal with first, it is important
that we get clear in our minds which of these problems we can do
something about and which ones we cannot. There's no point wasting our mental energy thinking about things we can do nothing
about. We want to use our energy to its maximum by focusing only
on what we can do something about. We need to separate our challenges (it's a more positive word than problems) into two groups;
ones we can do something about and ones we cannot. For example,
if you have been paid off or made redundant, there's nothing you can
do to change the fact that this has happened. You may not be happy
about it, but dwelling on it or focusing on it isn't going to change
anything. So what's the point? What you can dwell on is the solu-

tion. Once you have identified the problem (being made redundant), give 100 percent of your energy to the solution.

It's far better to be concentrating on the solution than dwelling on the problem. You cannot change the fact that you were made redundant, but you do have complete control over your attitude and over what you will do from that moment onward. There's no point trying to mentally fight the fact that it happened and wish it hadn't happened, because it has. This only wastes energy and increases stress. You need to accept the fact that this has happened, and the sooner you do, the sooner you will be at peace with yourself. That's the first step in overcoming anything: Accept what has happened.

The second step is to say to yourself: What can I do about it? Depending on what has happened, there may be something you can do about it or there may not. In the case of being made redundant, depending on your attitude, you could decide to use this as an opportunity to study a subject you've always been interested in but maybe didn't have the time before. Or you may decide that this would be a good time to go into a completely different line of work, perhaps with increased pay or better hours. Or you could decide to go into business for yourself so that you will never have to answer to a boss or be in a position where you can be fired. But whatever you decide to do, put it into action immediately. Don't procrastinate. This is the third step.

(1). Accept what has happened.
(2). What can I do about it?
(3). Begin immediately to put this plan into action.

Someone once said, "You don't have a problem, you only have a decision to make," and there is a fair bit of truth in that. But in the case of bad things happening to us which we can do nothing about, we just have to accept that it is so. We can either be bitter or get better, but we can't do both. But by being bitter, we can destroy both our bodies and our minds.

Procrastination

Procrastination is one of the biggest failure diseases there is. It is responsible for the loss of so many people's dreams because they decided to do tomorrow what they could've done to-day. But why put off until tomorrow what you are able to do today? Do you realise there is energy released in doing something now? By doing something now, it actually makes you feel more energetic. By the same token, putting something off actually makes you feel less energetic. This is actually a mental disease more than a physical one, but as we have already mentioned, the mental affects the physical. It basically comes down to a lack of dis-cipline, and it can easily develop into a habit. If you procrastinate once, then it's very easy to procrastinate again, and before you know where you are, things are not being accomplished that should be getting accomplished— and guess what happens to your levels of stress?

That's right; your stress level goes up. The more things you put off, the more things you have weighing on your mind. This also drains some of your energy, which certainly doesn't help. The only way to get rid of this self-defeating habit is to actively force yourself to do something now. Just as you can get into a habit of procrastinating, so can you get into a habit of doing something now. In fact, it's just as easy to develop the habit of doing something now as it is to get into the failure habit of procrastinating. You will find that as you force yourself to do something now, you will have more enthusiasm about doing the next thing, and you will also be happier and feel better about yourself. The thought of doing some-thing you are not looking forward to is actually worse than doing it. Have you ever noticed that once you have started, it's not quite as bad as you thought? This is because your mind has a tendency to blow things out of proportion and exaggerate them.

Someone once said that the richest place in town is not the bank but the graveyard, because there you will find so many people who died without accomplishing their dreams. Books that were nev-er written, songs that were never sung, businesses that were nev-er started, ideas that were never acted upon, dreams that were never fulfilled, the list could go on and on, but sadly "most people go to their graves with the music still in them," (Anonymous).

We all have a limited amount of time on this planet and not one of us knows how long that will be. So why even waste one day— or one hour? By procrastinating, not only do you increase stress, but it is also a waste of valuable time. Once we waste some time, whether it's a day or an hour or even a minute, it is gone forever and we can never get that back again. Part of our life has been squandered.

But please don't confuse having some genuine time off or having a break with procrastinating. They are totally different. In fact, when you are working hard it is essential to have some time off now and again, otherwise you would burn yourself out. People who work long hard hours and don't have enough time off will be in danger of having high stress levels, which can eventually affect their physical health. There has to be a sensible balance between hard work and regular time off, and it's up to us as individuals to figure out what feels best for us. For example, I know someone who has a day job working for a boss Monday to Friday, and they also have their own part time business, which they work in the evenings, during the week. But when it comes to the weekend, they're off and it's well deserved because they've worked hard all week. Not only do they feel they deserve it, but it gives them something to look forward to and re-energises them for the week ahead.

The old saying is very true, "All work and no play makes Jack a dull boy." We need to reward ourselves for our efforts, and this will keep us motivated, energised, and enthusiastic.

Don't Be Your Own Worst Enemy

Sometimes we cause ourselves unnecessary stress by our habits, our attitudes, and the words we speak. Untidiness or clutter at home or in our workspace can add to stress. Have you ever noticed that the more stuff or clutter we have lying around, the more stressed we seem to be? There seems to be a direct relationship between our state of mind and the state of our environment. So it's important to be organised and to file things away so you know where everything is. If you're not using something, put it away, wherever it belongs. Get rid of things you don't need. If there are things that someone else could use, such as clothes, CDs, books, unwanted gifts, etc., why not give them away to charity? By doing this you'll be helping someone else as well as yourself. The general rule of thumb is, if you haven't used something in a year, then you'll probably won't use it again. By getting rid of the old, you also make room for the new. So clear your environment and clear your mind.

Another thing that can happen to us is that people or situations can "steal" our attitude, but only if we let them. No one or nothing can steal our attitude unless we first give them permission to take it. In other words, we decide to react negatively. Suppose you were walking past someone and you said to them, "Good morning," and they ignored you. What would your attitude be? Would you feel angry or would you rise above it and not let it bother you?

If you got angry then that person has stolen your attitude. But if you decide not to let it bother you, then you are a bigger person than they are, and you are still in possession of your attitude. Don't let people or situations control you by dictating how you will feel. Stay in control of yourself, and remember, your attitude is valuable so don't let anyone steal it.

It's also important to make sure that you get enough sleep. Lack of sleep can cause moodiness and irritability and can add to your stress levels. It also affects your ability to concentrate. The amount of sleep required will vary for everybody. Some people need seven or eight hours sleep, while others will happily get by on four or five hours sleep. I personally used to be convinced I needed eight hours sleep, but I have realised since that I can function just as effectively on six. I'm not saying this is the case for everybody. I can only speak for myself, but it's up to you to figure out what feels best for you. This is what I call the optimum amount. The optimum amount simply means the minimum amount of sleep required while still being able to function and operate with maximum effectiveness.

Sleep is very important for our wellbeing and our ability to function effectively. Once we know what our optimum amount of sleep is, it's important that we don't go below that amount, at least not on a regular basis, otherwise we will suffer from fatigue.

There are many things which take place during sleep. For example, the body renews itself, our muscles are rested, our heartbeat slows down, and our breathing becomes shallower. The healing process and other subconscious activities can take place more rapidly because there is no interference from our conscious minds. If we deny ourselves the sleep we need, then these vital processes get disrupted, and as a result we suffer from stress and fatigue. In order to operate with maximum effectiveness, physically and mentally, we need to get enough sleep.

Some people unknowingly make things harder for themselves by the words they speak. For example, suppose they were out on the road late at night and they didn't get home until 3 o'clock in the morning and they were due to get up for work again at 6:30 A.M. What would most people tell themselves? That's right! Most people would tell themselves, "I'm going to be shattered tomorrow because I'm hardly going to get any sleep tonight and I'm up early for work in the morning." And as a result of saying that, they are shattered the next day. Is it any surprise? Not really, because their subconscious mind picks up what they've just said and takes it as a command and sees to it that they are shattered. Yes, I realise this person probably went below their optimum amount of sleep, but sometimes we might find ourselves in situations where it's unavoidable. If we do find ourselves in situations like this, then telling ourselves negative things and giving ourselves negative affirmations isn't going to help; it's only going to make us feel worse. So why do it? Remember, your subconscious mind doesn't know the difference between truth and falsehood, so if you were to tell yourself the next morning that you felt great because you had eight hours sleep, even although it wasn't true, you would feel a lot better than if you told yourself you were shattered because you only got about three and a half hours sleep. Although you consciously knew you didn't get eight hours sleep, that is just an example of how the subconscious can be tricked into believing whatever you tell it. Even if you did feel slightly fatigued, it is still better to be speaking positive words than negative words.

The Mind-Body Connection

It's a proven fact that 80 percent to 90 percent of all ailments are stress-related. What does that tell us? It means that if we can get rid of stress, or at least reduce it considerably, then maybe we can get rid of or reduce many of our ailments. Most of our physical maladies are created by what goes on in our minds. There is even growing evidence to support the argument that potentially fatal diseases, such as cancer, first originate in the mind. It is not the purpose of this book to say whether it does or doesn't, only to point out that our minds can create either health or sickness in our physical bodies.

This part of the book really refers to minor ailments, such as the common cold, and how people can sometimes unknowingly "feed" such ailments and reinforce them by their words and their actions. We must remember that our subconscious mind is the builder of our bodies and it is we who give direction to our subconscious by our thoughts, attitudes, words, and actions. As Dr. Joseph Murphy states in his book The Power of your Subconscious Mind, illness and disease are abnormal. It is normal to be healthy and it is abnormal to be sick. God didn't create us sick, He created us well. Neither did He create us with negative emotions or thoughts. Every thought we think, every word we speak, and every emotion we have has a corresponding effect on our physical bodies.

When our thoughts and emotions are negative, it disrupts and prevents the subconscious from operating harmoniously, which in turn weakens our immune system and leaves us more vulnerable to catching disease or becoming ill. Worry is also a major contributor to feeling stressed, but there are ways to combat worry. For example, you could become so busy that you don't have time to worry; in other words, you could crowd it out by involving yourself in worthwhile causes or projects. There's nothing worse than sitting at home alone with nothing to look at but four walls. These are the danger moments as far as worry is concerned, because it's when you are alone or have nothing to keep yourself occupied with that your mind is free to wander.

A lot of worry stems from being self-focused, so why not become others-focused and take an interest in other people? Find out what's going on in their lives and what their dreams and ambitions are. Why not get out of the house and join a club, or become involved at your church, or start your own part-time business? Anything that involves mixing with other people in a worthwhile cause will help you shift the focus off yourself and onto them. You will find that as you do this and you become busier, eventually worry will be crowded out and it will no longer have a place in your life.

Most people are unaware that illness and ailments thrive on recognition. The more attention you give something, the bigger it becomes in your own mind. When you give something more recognition that it deserves, you actually help to keep it alive. For example, have you ever heard someone repeatedly go on about the terrible cold they have and they just can't seem to get rid of it? Of course there may be physical factors involved too, but repeatedly talking about it and giving it undue attention will only help to prolong it.

I'm not saying we can rid ourselves of all ailments and diseases, but I do believe that by speaking positive words, thinking positive thoughts, and renewing our minds on a daily basis, we can strengthen our immune systems and certainly help to reduce the effects of some minor ailments. Here's how it works:

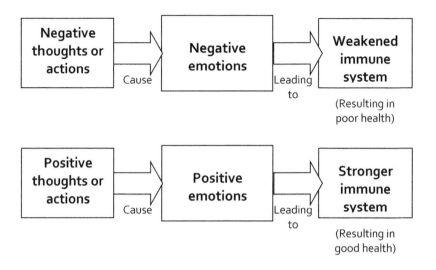

Our emotions are really a subconscious response to our conscious thinking, which in turn will lead to either good health or poor health. It's amazing how many physicians today will treat the symptoms of a disease but will completely ignore the root cause, which is their thinking. I'm not saying all illness is caused by negative thinking or emotions, but if it is, giving a person a pill or tablet may offer some temporary relief at best, but it's not going to solve the root cause of a psychosomatic problem. Obviously our diet plays a vitally important part in our well-being, but that is not the purpose of this book.

The vast majority of people don't realise the power of the words they speak. When you speak about something you give it life. By that I mean within the realms of your own mind. You can create a state of mind within yourself that did not exist before, simply by speaking words. If you were to say, "I've got a cold," or "I feel terrible," you are creating an extremely negative state of mind within yourself. How can you hope to feel better if you are affirming something negative? Not only is it a negative affirmation, but you are giving it life. Think about it. If speaking about something gives it life, then surely the opposite must hold true, that not speaking about it, or even better, speaking words of health, could help to kill it off. Remember what the book of Proverbs says, *"The tongue has the power of life and death"* (Prov. 18:21).

Some people might say, "But I really do have a cold, I'm only telling the truth." Well, that may be true but affirming that you've got a cold or how bad you feel is only going to make it more definite to your subconscious mind and help to prolong it. The more attention or recognition you give something, the more power it has over you, but you could, if you wish, choose to give it no recognition. For example, if someone said, "How are you today?" you could say "Fantastic," or, "Great," and not even mention that you had a cold, and because of a lack of recognition your subconscious may start to assume that all is well and bring about a more speedy recovery.

If you have a cold and someone comments, "I see you have a bit of a cold," obviously you're not going to lie or deny it, but you could play it down by saying, "It's almost gone," or, "It's nothing much, it's on its way out," thus reducing its power over you. That's a whole lot better than saying, "Yeah, it's terrible. I've had it for two weeks and I just can't get rid of it."

Another way we give ailments power over us is by giving them a name. By naming something, we recognise its existence. Our job, if you like, is to convince our subconscious mind it doesn't exist, and the only way to do that is to starve it of all recognition. If we give our ailments a name, such as "a cold" or "the flu," it automatically produces a vivid mental picture in our minds and makes a bigger impact on our subconscious. Although we may still have the symptoms or the ailment, refusing to acknowledge it and give it a name will lessen the impact on your subconscious mind.

Recognition by Actions

We recognise our ailments not only by our words but also by our actions. Remember that actions as well as words control your inner self-talk and influence your subconscious mind. Every action you take is picked up by your subconscious mind, which responds accordingly. For example, if you have a cold and you take a pill, the very act of taking a pill reinforces to your subconscious that you must be ill. Your subconscious associates' medicine and pills with illness, and this action therefore directs your inner self-talk toward that of being ill, thus giving the ailment more power over you. By your very actions you have recognised the existence of an ailment. This is one of the ways in which the subconscious works, by means of association. By that I mean it associates things with other things. Obviously this is one such example, but another example of the subconscious working by association could be to do with memories you have that are associated with a certain piece of music.

It's true you may like a certain piece of music, but it's also true that you like the memories or thoughts it causes you to think. Your subconscious mind associates a particular piece of music with certain memories or events that happened in your life. Notice that you did not consciously try to make this association, but it happened automatically by the workings of your subconscious mind. The subconscious is always trying to make sense out of things and put them in order, and this is one way in which it tries to achieve this.

If your doctor or physician has recommended some kind of medication, or told you to do, or not to do something, for goodness sake listen to them and take their advice. I am only explaining what has worked for me and can make no guarantees for any other person.

Some people also give additional power to their ailments by letting them control their behaviour. For example someone may have a slight touch of the cold and decide to cancel their night out, or they may have been planning to go out a walk with their partner and decided not to because they have a cold. In other words, they give major recognition to their ailments and even further power to them by allowing them to control their lifestyle. Their subconscious then picks this behaviour up and accepts that they must be ill— otherwise they wouldn't be acting this way— and proceeds accordingly, thereby feeding the ailment. Is it then any surprise if it does get worse or if they do have a hard time shaking it off? Now don't get me wrong, I know there are people who are genuinely ill, who physically aren't able to do certain things, and that's not what I'm referring to; but people who only have a very slight touch of something and are still energetic enough to be able to carry on as normal.

Please note that for these techniques to work, everything must add up. By that I mean you can't be sending mixed messages to your subconscious mind. Suppose, for example, you were speaking positive words and were affirming good health but were also taking medication at the same time. Your subconscious would be receiving mixed messages and this would reduce the chances of your subconscious working in your favour. Remember, actions speak louder than words, especially to your subconscious.

People also contribute to the ageing process by telling themselves they're getting old. I'm sure we've all heard people make comments such as, "It's a sign of old age," or, "I'm getting too old for that." The more times people repeat these statements, the more ingrained these thought processes will become in their subconscious mind. What else can we expect the subconscious to do except obey these commands?

Some people may say "but I'm only joking," but remember, the subconscious doesn't take a joke; it simply acts upon everything you say whether you are serious or not.

Just as an example, when you hear the word pension, what kind of picture does this conjure up in your mind? Is it one of good health, physical fitness, and prosperity? Or is it a picture that is not quite so appealing? I think you get the point, don't you? What about the words old age pension? What kind of picture does that conjure up? Does it make the picture in your mind a little bit gloomier? Remember the words you speak creates mental images in your mind. As Maxwell Maltz states in his book Psycho Cybernetics, the pictures you continuously hold in your mind are what your subconscious takes as a goal and is constantly working on to achieve. Although we speak in words, our mind thinks in pictures. For example, if someone says the word tiger, we don't picture in our minds the five letters of the word, we picture the actual tiger itself.

Of course there are other factors involved in the ageing process too, and of course we are all ageing whether we like it or not, but why contribute to the process if we don't have to? The danger is that by speaking words of getting old, it can lead to actions which support this belief. This only makes an even deeper impression on your subconscious mind and contributes to the vicious cycle. For example, someone might say that they're too old to start their own business or they might turn down a chance to go somewhere with their friends because they think they are too old.

Some people even allow age to dictate what kind of clothes they wear. In other words they let age control their lifestyle to a large degree. I'm not saying whether people should or shouldn't do something, because that is completely up to them, but we should bear in mind that every single thing we do or don't do is picked up by our subconscious mind. If the inner self-talk or reason behind it is "I'm getting old," then this is what will be accepted by the subconscious mind and this is what it will work onto achieve. I often wonder what kind of effect retirement has on the subconscious mind, because this also sends a very definite and powerful message to your subconscious mind that you have now reached a certain stage in life. Sadly, the statistics show that many people don't live very long after retirement. It's obvious retirement has a powerful effect on your inner self-talk and how you feel about your-self, and personally I don't want to ever retire. I'm not saying I don't want holidays or time off, of course I do, but I don't want to ever be in a position where I've stopped working completely.

It's important to have dreams and goals in front of you all the time, because life without dreams or goals is a mere existence and dull at best. It stands to reason that if the ageing process can be sped up, it must be able to be slowed down. You can't have a plus without a minus, and you can't have a minus without a plus. I often wonder what would happen if we gave our subconscious different messages and told it the opposite. Obviously we can't stop the ageing process, but we can certainly stack everything in our favor. Instead of saying, "I'm too old for that," what if we used the affirmation, "Every day I'm getting younger and younger?" Although this is an impossibility, it doesn't matter because the subconscious will act upon it just the same, and it will certainly be a lot more beneficial than telling ourselves that we're getting older and older. Suppose also that we never ever retired, but our work was well punctuated with regular time off and holidays. Would our subconscious know we had reached a certain age? Would it be directed differently? Would it produce different results in our lives? Who knows?

Remember, the mind is like a computer, and the signals that reach it constantly will eventually be expressed in your life in actual physical reality.

CHAPTER FIVE

TV (and its influence)

The television is a fantastic invention and is the source of a lot of entertainment for many people, but like most things, there are advantages and disadvantages regarding television. Although TV can give us enjoyment at times, it is also responsible for controlling our thoughts, emotions, and our time. It can even influence the words we speak as a result of what we are watching. I must also point out that TV itself isn't bad, it's what's being programmed into our minds that matters.

There are many things on TV that are very interesting and positive, but even so, too much of that can still have an adverse affect in our lives by eating away at our time and side-tracking us from what we really want in our lives, our dreams. Most people, through ignorance of how the mind works, are not aware of the psychological effects of TV. They may be aware of the amount of time they spend in front of the TV but not so much of the effect. Think about it. If a two minute advert can cause someone to go out and buy something, what effect could a two-hour film have on them? The TV has an extremely powerful effect on our psyche and our emotions. Too many times we have seen crimes committed as a result of what someone has watched on TV. Regardless of what anyone else says, TV affects us whether we like it or not or believe it or not. The reason for this is that when you watch TV, you can't help thinking about what you are watching, therefore it is controlling your thoughts. Many people at this very moment are being controlled by TV without realising they are being controlled. When you are watching something on TV, the TV is doing your thinking for you and you have no control over what you will see next. Therefore it would be fair to say that to a certain degree, you are out of control of your thoughts. Whatever appears on the screen next is what you will think about. It's almost as if the TV is saying to you, "Now you will think about this, and then you will think about this," and so on, all the way through. Therefore, you really have to decide if you are going to control the TV or if it is going to control you.

If you switch on the TV every day, simply out of habit, then the TV is probably controlling you. The first thing some people do when they get up in the morning is turn on the TV, and when they come home in the evening they switch on the TV regardless of what's on. Now that's all very well if that's all you want out of life, but if you want to achieve your dreams and goals, then you're going to have to develop some new habits and get rid of some old habits. You need to ask yourself, is this action (and this could relate to anything, not just TV) going to take me closer to my dreams or further away from them? If the answer is further away, then this is a habit you need to break, because it's holding you back. You need to re-member that the TV has an on/off switch and that you are ultimately in control of the TV. Why not listen to some of your favourite music instead? Not only will this put you in a more positive frame of mind, but it will also free up a lot of your time to do things you would nev-er have accomplished while watching TV. It will also force you to think and to be more creative. You may be surprised at the amount of new ideas you get as a result of changing what goes into your mind.

The TV is also responsible for controlling your emotions, be-cause when you see something on TV whether it's good or bad, your thoughts create an emotional response in your body.

DANGERS OF TV:
CONTROLS YOUR THOUGHTS
CONTROLS YOUR EMOTIONS
LIMITS CREATIVE THINKING
TIME WASTER
CONVERSATION KILLER
DREAM STEALER

Think of all the different emotions you may experience by watching the news on TV. Ask yourself what emotions you would feel as a result of watching the following:

- A terrorist attack.
- A rumour of a deadly disease in your home town.
- A convicted murderer gets only a few months in jail.
- Someone you know winning the lottery.
- Your country may be going to war.
- A gloomy weather forecast.

- A politician making a speech about something you completely disagree with.

How do you feel now? Fired up? Motivated? Probably not, and it's hardly surprising. Think of all the negative emotions and thoughts you have just experienced, all because of a little screen in the corner of the room. I'm not saying there isn't the occasional piece of good news, but the vast majority of what's on TV is negative. So how do you know if something is positive or negative? Well, a good guide is to check your emotions. If something is causing you to have negative emotions, it's negative. Why watch something that's going to pull you down and make you feel bad? How can you ever hope to become successful in life and achieve your dreams while entertaining such negative emotions? You need to be in control of your thoughts and emotions on a daily basis. You need to avoid negative emotions like the plague, and the best way to avoid the negative is by putting positive in. It's going to be hard enough to achieve your dreams and goals without making even it harder for yourself.

Some people still claim TV doesn't affect them, but people who say that usually don't realise the difference between the conscious and the subconscious mind. They may say things like, "I can watch TV and it doesn't cause me to go out and murder," and yes, that may be true, it may not cause them to go out and murder, but what they are referring to is their conscious thinking (where we make decisions) and not the subconscious, which is the most powerful part.

If these same people were to watch a gruesome bloody film, if they liked it or not, their emotions would be affected just the same as any other person. It wouldn't matter how hard they consciously tried not to let it affect them, it would because when the conscious and subconscious are in conflict, the subconscious (where our emotions come from) always wins. Remember, the subconscious doesn't know the difference between a real experience and one vividly imagined; therefore; when you watch something on TV, your subconscious responds emotionally, just as if it were really happening. That's why people get scared when they go to see a creepy movie. Although our conscious mind knows there is no real threat or danger, it is still very real to our subconscious mind.

Another reason TV has such a powerful effect on us is that it engages two of our senses, both hearing and seeing. This has a much bigger effect on us than, for example, listening to a radio, which only involves using one of our senses. Not only that, but our minds retain a bigger percentage of what we see compared to what we hear.

Occasionally you hear some people say, "But you've got to watch the news, you need to know what's going on in the world." Well, I disagree. You do not need to know what's going on in the world. Now please, don't misunderstand me, I'm not saying that we shouldn't care or help people. Of course we should. I think we should do everything we possibly can to help other people, but watching negative events on TV is not going to help anybody else one little bit simply by watching it. It doesn't do you any good either; it only drags you down. So what's the point? Wouldn't it be far more beneficial to be giving something away financially than watching TV? That way, not only are your doing something constructive to help other people, but you will have a more positive state of mind yourself. Some people may argue that if we don't know what's going on, then we don't know who to give to, but remember that God commands us to give on a regular basis, regardless of what's happening in the world. (This will be covered later in the book.)

It's hard for us as human beings to be of any great service to anyone while we are negative. We've got to fight to stay positive and that way we can help other people become positive. When you stop watching the news on TV, its amazing how much more uplifted you feel and how much happier you are. I can tell you from personal experience that when I first decided to cut out watching TV and stop listening to the radio, it was like a huge weight being lifted off my shoulders. Life seemed so much brighter again and the world seemed like a good place to be. Remember, our minds have no choice but to feed off what we allow into it, and we are the ones who make that choice. The truth is, the world is a good place to be. If you watch the news on TV or listen to events on the radio, you will probably be convinced otherwise, but remember, all the doom and gloom you hear about happening in the world, compared to all the good things, makes up a very small percentage of the total picture. It's just that we don't usually hear much about the good things happening.

Although negative events happening in the world represent a very small percentage of the total picture, it can become 100 percent of what's going on in our minds of that's all we focus on. As a result of this we can easily become convinced that the whole world is bad.

Focus

If you are watching negative events on TV on a regular basis, then that will become your focus. These negative thoughts and emotions will start to dominate your thinking. The problem with this is that you cannot be focusing on the positive and the negative at the same time. If you are focusing on negative events, then you will lose sight of the positive, and if you cut out focusing on negative events, then you will automatically gravitate towards the positive. You could compare it to looking through a camera lens. Imagine you had a beautiful garden and you decided to go out and take some photographs. Now suppose you had lovely flowers and plants and this took up about 95 percent of your total garden area, but over in the corner there were some weeds. What would you take photos of and what would you focus on? Why? Would you focus on what was good about your garden or what was bad about it? Would you focus on what was right about it or what was wrong with it? Imagine you were going to show these photographs to some of your colleagues at work who had never seen your garden before and you decided to photograph only the weeds and nothing else. You take the photos in to work and pass them around. What kind of impression do you think they will have of your garden? Why? Of course they will have a bad impression of it because that's 100 percent of what they know about it, even although it's only 5 percent of the true picture. Is it an accurate impression of your garden? Absolutely not, because you know you have a beautiful garden and the vast majority of your garden is well kept and looks great, but you decided not to focus on any of that, so subsequently that's all that came out in the photographs. Understand that when you watch the news or negative events on TV, it's like focusing on the weeds. Why would you want to do that when there are so many good things you could focus on?

Frequency

Most people watch TV or listen to the radio every day. Not only is it every day, but it is usually for several hours every day. Can you imagine how powerful an effect this has on your mind? Although the TV is more powerful than the radio, the radio is still powerful nevertheless. You may only be using one of your senses, but that is powerful enough to give direction and focus to your thinking. When you put on the radio just out of habit, it still dictates to you what you will think about. You have no control over what you will hear next; therefore, the radio is really deciding what you will think about, and most of it is negative. You still hear about all the terrible events and crimes that are happening, and if you have the radio on for long periods of time, you will probably hear these same events over and over several times in one day. These negative events will then become firmly embedded in your subconscious mind, and this will become your focus. For example how do you feel when you hear about traffic jams, a five car pile-up, a gloomy weather forecast, or some terrible crime? What emotions would you be experiencing? Will listening to that take you any closer to your dreams or goals? Will it motivate you? If you are listening to the radio early in the morning, what frame of mind will it put you in for the day ahead? Positive or negative? The general rule of thumb is, if it doesn't motivate you it's not positive. If you are listening to someone on the radio and you either disagree or don't like what they're saying, your emotions will be negative if you like it or not, because it happens automatically. So why do it?

Most people put on the radio and TV simply out of habit because that's all they've been used to. For most of their lives they've watched TV and listened to the radio on a daily basis, so consequently they don't know what it's like not to have TV and radio in their lives and mentally they have no comparison. Television and radio not only affect your focus but also affect your attitude and your outlook in life.

If you are listening to or watching negative stuff regularly, then you will start to develop a more pessimistic attitude toward life in general, as a result of what has gone into your mind. Just as surely as water seeks its own level, so will what you put into your mind come out in one way or another. Have you ever noticed that whatever someone continually focuses on is what they talk about most of the time?

Don't get me wrong, there's nothing wrong with talking about your interests or hobbies if that's your focus, but the danger is when you start to focus on and talk about negative things. Remember, words are affirmations, and as a result of watching TV one can easily end up programming their subconscious mind with negative words.

Have you ever spoken words of anger in response to what was on TV? It may have been some kind of injustice, or anything at all for that matter, but that little screen in the corner was allowed to control your words, your emotions, and your attitude.

Here's how it works:

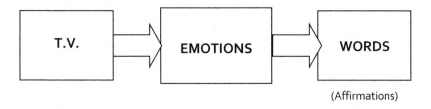

(Affirmations)

Whatever you watch on TV you find yourself thinking about and talking about. For example, someone may have seen something negative on TV the night before and this will be the topic of conversation the next day, perhaps even several times a day. What happens the next night? Yes, you've guessed it, they see something else negative and this becomes fuel for their next conversation. Before long their whole focus is doom and gloom and what's wrong with the world.

All this is picked up by their subconscious mind and starts to dominate their thinking and affect their emotions. As a result they have a lot of negative emotions that they carry around on a daily basis unnecessarily. Don't get me wrong, I'm not saying they are not good people, but through ignorance of how the mind works they have fallen prey to the effects of TV.

The Law of Attraction

What you focus on is what you attract. The law of attraction applies to every one of us whether we like it or not or believe it or not. The law is that whatever the most dominant thoughts are in our minds we will attract to ourselves in actual physical reality. In other words we will attract to ourselves that which we think about most. It's as real as the law of gravity or the law of cause and effect. Like the law of gravity, it makes no difference if we believe in it or not; if we jump off a cliff, we are going to fall and we will soon find out that it applies to us just the same as it applies to anyone else.

Please understand before I go any further that the law of attraction isn't necessarily bad. It's actually neutral. It's just as possible to attract good things and good people as it is to attract bad things and bad people. Whether we attract the good or attract the bad depends upon what's going on in our minds. If our thoughts and emotions are positive, we will attract the positive, but if our thoughts and emotions are negative, we will attract the negative. Just as surely as night follows day, eventually our most dominant thoughts will start to manifest themselves in actual physical reality.

Most people are not even aware that there is such a thing as a law of attraction, but the truth is it is operating in all of our lives all the time. Have you ever noticed that when our state of mind is positive and we feel "on top of the world," everything seems to go right and we seem to attract other positive people? Consequently, when our state of mind is negative and we are suffering from negative emotions, nothing seems to go right and we seem to attract other negative people. The truth is that we are always attracting people with similar states of mind to our own. Who we are is who we attract. It's almost as if we are magnets. In a sense, the subconscious mind is like a magnet in that it is always attracting something. Life is like a mirror, and we see the world and other people in it as we see ourselves.

Some people find themselves watching negative programs such as "How to Beat the Burglar" and they watch these programs regularly. As a result, thoughts of being burgled start to dominate their thinking and they live their lives in fear. Some people, if they watch these programs often enough, can actually end up expecting to be burgled. If watching these programs becomes a regular pattern and a regular part of their conversation, then these thoughts of being burgled will be very dominant in their subconscious mind. Through ignorance of how the mind works, they are unaware that the law of attraction is always in force.

Words Create, Words Attract

The subconscious is a goal-seeking mechanism and the words we speak have the power to create and to attract whatever we speak about. That's why we need to be very careful about the words that habitually come out of our mouths. The more we speak about something, the more life we give it and the higher the chance of attracting it. Our state of mind is constantly attracting things to us, but our words create our state of mind.

Here's how it works:

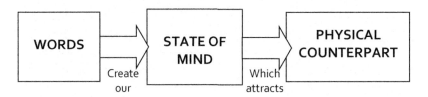

Once again, this law is neutral. We are all responsible for the words we speak, and if we are wise we will use this to our advantage. We must always be speaking about what we want to happen, not what we fear might happen.

I'm not saying that watching these programs once or twice will cause you to be burgled, but only if these thoughts are deep rooted and long-held will it increase the chances of attracting it. The Bible clearly warns us of the principle of attracting what we dwell upon: *"What I feared has come upon me, what I dreaded has happened to me"* (Job 3:25).

It's really just a question of what we choose to dwell on. What do you dwell on the most, success or failure? Why not use this same principle to your advantage and use it to attract what you want; your dream? That's exactly what successful people do, and it's exactly the reason you need to write down your goals or have pictures of your dreams where you can see them every day. When you see these pictures every day— suppose for example it was a red Porsche— then this red Porsche will start to dominate your thinking at a subconscious level. Even if you don't have enough money to buy one just now, you will attract opportunities which will put you in a position to have the money. How the subconscious brings something about or attracts it is none of our business; it has powers we know nothing about. It's only our job to present it with the idea or goal, and it will go to work to bring it about.

Creative Imagination

It's a proven fact that creative people live longer. People such as musicians, artists, inventors, poets, writers, etc., have demonstrated that by using more of our creative imagination we can lengthen our lives. Although our bodies may eventually show signs of wear, the mind itself never gets old. I believe the old saying is true, "You're only as old as you think you are." It's so easy to mentally get into a rut where we no longer really have to use our creative imagination. Life can easily become dull and mundane if we allow our minds to stagnate.

I believe that using our creative imagination adds an extra dimension to life and helps us to stay enthusiastic. When you are using your creative imagination, whether it's to design something or create something or whatever, there is no room for boredom because you have a goal and a purpose and it puts the excitement back into life. The problem with TV is that while you are watching it, you are forming the habit of not using your creative imagination. The more TV you watch, the less your creative imagination is being used, and you can easily fall into a rut mentally. Remember, the more we force ourselves to think, the more we are able to think; the less we force ourselves to think, the less we are able to think. It's almost like keeping fit mentally. The more you exercise your mind, the more your mind is able to do. It was the creative imagination that great thinkers such as Thomas Edison relied on in helping him to develop the electric light bulb.

There have even been cases of children whose grades started to improve in school as a result of playing chess. Obviously because they were playing chess they were being forced to use their creative imagination. When you use your creative imagination in one area, it has a tendency to affect other areas of your life. Because they were becoming more creative by playing chess, mentally there was a carry-over and they found themselves being more creative at school as well.

Spectator or Participant?

While you are watching TV you are a spectator in life rather than a participant. The people you are watching on TV are participants in their game of life and are living their dreams. At some point in life, they decided they wanted to pursue a dream, and the only way to accomplish that was to get up and do something. Some people remain spectators their whole lives, and there's nothing wrong with that if that's all they want out of life, but if they want more than that then they're going to have to get rid of some old habits and develop some success habits instead. People who become successful decide to become participants in the game of life and are willing to change their habits. They realise that some habits are beneficial and others are detrimental to their success.

You will find that any truly successful person you talk to didn't get there by accident. They had to work hard, discipline themselves, and make some sacrifices along the way. In other words, they had to go through some pain to get there. These are words that usually scare the average person off. That's why average people are average and truly successful people are in the minority. Remember, no pain, no gain.

It's really a case of priorities. What's more important to you, your dream or TV? Are you willing to make some changes and become what you are capable of becoming, or do you want to be enslaved by TV your whole life? Realise the TV has the potential to steal your dream, but only if you let it. You alone make that choice. You wouldn't be reading this book just now if I was still in the habit of watching TV or was unwilling to change any of my old habits.

I could've allowed the TV to steal my dream, but I got fed up being a spectator in life and wanted to be a participant. I am just one person, but how many people are out there whose dreams will never ever be fulfilled because of TV? People who had great potential but never fully realised it because they allowed TV to dominate their lives.

People who could've achieved so much but were content to watch other people achieving instead. We will probably never know how many peoples' dreams have been stolen by TV, but my guess is that it would be quite a substantial figure.

TV Can Steal Your Life

Assuming most people watch TV every day, how many hours per day would you say the average person watches TV? Two hours? Four hours? Six hours?

Let's say for the sake of the example that you watch TV four hours per day on average. That's a sixth of every day spent looking at a little screen in the corner of the room. A sixth may not sound much, but two months out of every year— which you can never ever get back—is being used up by watching TV. That's quite a bit! Now let's be really optimistic and say that you lived to be a hundred and twenty years of age. Do you realise that twenty years of your life would have been spent sitting looking at a TV screen? Do you want to waste twenty years? Think what else you could have accomplished with those twenty years? You may say, "Yeah, but I'm not planning to live until a hundred and twenty." Well, that's fine, but why waste even one year?

If you want to achieve your dreams, then you need to seriously ask yourself if you really want to be wasting two months per year of your valuable time. Remember, if you value life, then you should value time, because time is the stuff of which life is made. I've never heard of anyone yet who was on their death bed and when asked if they could live their lives over again, what would they do differently? Say they wished they'd spent more time watching TV. In fact, when a survey was carried out to interview people who had reached a hundred years of age, they were all asked that same question, and the vast majority of them replied, "I wish I'd taken more risks." That answer kind of puts TV in its proper perspective, doesn't it? But the chances are you've got a heck of a long way to go before you reach a hundred, so why not do something now while time is on your side? Why not learn from their mistakes?

Personally, when I used to watch TV, I only watched about two hours per day on average, but I have since found about an extra four hours in my day. How is that, you might ask? Because remember in a previous chapter I said that I cut my sleep down from eight hours per day to six and found I could function just as well on six. I benefited from an extra two hours per day from sleeping less and a further two hours per day from cutting out TV, so each day I am four hours better off I than I was. Obviously I still have the same amount of hours in my day, but as a result of making a few changes, I have increased my productivity and accomplish a whole lot more than I used to.

Some people, when presented with an opportunity to improve their lifestyle, claim they don't have the time to do anything else, but very often these same people will sit in front of the TV for hours on end and may even find time to read the newspaper. So it's not a case of having the time or not having the time; it's a case of priorities. What's more important to you? That's what we really need to ask ourselves.

Controlled Viewing if You Must

The reason I have included this part is because I realise some people may have certain things that interest them and this may provide a form of relaxation for them. For example, I have an interest in military history and you may have an interest in something else which appears on TV. It may even be something connected to your dreams. Suppose, for example, one of your dreams was to visit a certain group of islands in the Pacific Ocean and there was a documentary on about these group of islands. In that case it would be good to watch that program because it would be positive motivation and would fuel your desire to succeed. Some people may even use this as a form of dream building or switching off now and again. But even then, the amount of hours watched still needs to be limited to a certain amount if you are to achieve your dreams in life.

I realise it may not be easy for you to have total control over the TV especially if you have a family or husband or wife to think about. Although you might want to pursue your dreams and cut out watching TV, they might not feel the same way. Controlled viewing means that the TV doesn't get switched on just for the sake of switching it on. It only goes on if there is something in particular someone wants to watch, and as soon as that is finished, the TV goes right back off again. If there is nothing in particular that anyone wants to watch, then the TV stays off. Although this new habit might cause a few groans initially in your household, it's a good feeling when you start to take control of the TV instead of letting it control you. This is a battle that is well worth winning and pays dividends. You actually start to feel in control of your life again. The TV is a good servant but a poor master. Some people have the TV on just for the sake of some background noise, but as long as you can still see it or hear it, then subconsciously it is still having an effect on your mind. Remember, the subconscious picks up far more than we are consciously aware of.

Another alternative is to have a TV room. It all depends how disciplined you want to be, but I've known people who were pursuing their dreams and got rid of their TV completely because it was only going to be an obstacle to their dreams. Others weren't quite so extreme but decided that they would create a TV room instead. This room was specifically for watching TV only. The TV was taken out of the living room and put into another room, which would be called the TV room. This was the only room in the house with a TV, and the door was kept locked. Obviously the reason it was kept locked was that they had children. The mother and father weren't trying to be cruel or unfair, but they were actually doing it out of love, because they knew about the dangers of either too much TV or too much of the wrong stuff on TV. The children could use the TV room if they wanted to, but they first had to get Mum and Dad's permission. They had to say what they wanted to watch, and if Mum and Dad thought that what they wanted to see was suitable, then they were allowed to watch TV until that program was finished. The TV was then switched back off and the door was locked again. Obviously they let the children out first! The children now had to be creative if they liked it or not and were in a position where they were forced to think.

Remember, when it comes to the human mind, children are much more susceptible to input than adults. Children are in their formative years and, depending on what age they are, much of their self-image and their beliefs are still being formed. Don't you want to give them as much positive reinforcement as possible? On the other hand, if you have obedient children, you may not need to create a TV room. You may be content to keep it in the living room, where it is just now, so it's up to you. These are only suggestions and ideas, but ultimately you have to decide for yourself.

The Influence of TV on Behaviour

As we mentioned earlier, TV does influence our behaviour. If you don't think TV affects what people do, then why do companies and businesses spend millions of pounds each year on advertising? The reason they do that is because they know how easily the mind can be influenced by what people see on TV. They know the emotional impact TV can have on us. Usually in the case of advertising, it is to appeal to our emotion of desire, which in turn can cause us to take action, such as buy a product. Unfortunately it is not always the positive emotions that cause people to act. Sometimes people are motivated in a negative way as a result of what they watch.

Take, for example, a child who repeatedly watches violent films. Is it any surprise if he starts acting violently? It's no surprise at all because thoughts which constantly dominate our minds will eventually be expressed in one way or another. I'm sure we've all heard of crimes committed as result of what people saw on TV. But it doesn't necessarily have to be a crime that's committed; sometimes people are influenced by the language they hear or the lack of moral standards, or anything at all for that matter. If something is put into our minds often enough, it will eventually be accepted by our subconscious mind and this will become our new standard, regardless if it's right or wrong. All previous standards are then forgotten as this new standard takes its place. Even if the behaviour on TV is extremely violent or pornographic, if it is watched often enough, this behaviour will eventually be considered standard behaviour, or the norm.

Think of the changes that have taken place on TV in the last few decades. Things that are simply accepted now would have been considered outrageous twenty or thirty years ago.

To give you an example of how the mind will eventually accept what is put into it, I'm sure we are all familiar with speed bumps on our roads to slow down the traffic. I remember one neighbourhood that didn't have any speed bumps at all, and then suddenly the local council decided to put lots of speed bumps in that neighbourhood, on almost every street. At first there was uproar. Everyone was out complaining and people were phoning the council and writing letters, but the council said the bumps needed to be there, and to cut a long story short, the bumps are still there today. A few years later, people no longer complain because mentally they have accepted these speed bumps. The bumps which caused an outcry initially are the exact same bumps that don't bother them nearly as much today. The bumps haven't changed. The only thing that has changed is people's attitudes toward them, and they are now just considered a standard part of their daily living.

Is it any surprise that as moral standards on TV have declined or disappeared that the same thing has happened in society today? It doesn't come as any surprise at all, because over the years people have adjusted their standards and have accepted the standards they see on TV. It was once considered terrible if someone used a four-letter swear word on TV, but now it is commonplace and simply accepted as the norm. If children (or anyone at all, for that matter) are watching TV every day and are constantly bombarded with swear words, is it any surprise if they start swearing? Not really. What else are they supposed to think?

Remember, the key to firmly establishing something in your subconscious mind is repetition. The more frequent and more repetitive something is, the more embedded it gets. It is impossible to constantly put something into our minds and not eventually come out in one way or another.

CHAPTER SIX

The Solution (Part A)

"If you are wise, your wisdom will reward you."

(Proverbs 9:12)

This chapter is really the crux of the book. Although everything in this book is important, if you were to follow only the steps in this chapter alone, your life would improve dramatically. A lot of what is in this chapter has already been touched upon, but in this chapter I have attempted to define as clearly as possible a very simple but powerful system which I take absolutely no credit for but been fortunate enough to learn from other people who have helped me on my journey through life.

Although the system is simple, it is not easy - but there again, is life ever easy? Is anything worthwhile easy? No.

Sometimes things that are simple go unnoticed, or go in one ear and out the other; because people are always looking for some big complicated solution to solve their problems or they may even turn to drugs or alcohol to solve their problems, which of course, only makes things worse. The only thing that's going to solve your problems, apart from God Almighty is controlling what happens in the six inches between your ears. You won't find the solution externally. By that I mean you won't find it in money alone; you won't find it in material possessions; you won't find it at the local bar; and you won't find it by hanging around with negative people. Unfortunately, I don't think it's taught in schools either. Many people might simply overlook what's in this chapter because of the simplicity of it. They may be tempted to think, "Is that all there is to it?" and simply pass it by. But if you do that, then you've missed the whole point of this book.

The purpose of this book is to help you to improve your life by changing the way you think. If you want your outward life to change, then your inward life must change first, not the other way about. Because if you don't change, not much else will.

Your outward world will always be a reflection of your inner world. For example, if you had the belief that money was scarce, then that's exactly what you would see manifested in your physical world. Obviously the key is to control what goes into your mind on a constant daily basis. This means screening out the negative and only allowing positive input into your mind. If you do this long enough, slowly but surely your external world will start to change accordingly. But that's not what most people do, is it? Most people don't even think about what goes into their minds. Instead, they read newspapers, watch TV, and listen to the radio, and they may not even be aware that there is a better way to think. Well, I'm sorry if this sounds a bit blunt folks, but that kind of input is not going to get you anywhere in life. Most people are under the illusion that learning stops once they leave school or once they leave college or university. They think they pretty well know all they need to know to be able to go out and conquer the world, but nothing could be further from the truth. The truth is that none of us in our whole lives even come close to reaching our potential. American psychologist William James said, "Compared to what we ought to be, we are only half awake," and even that is being patronising. Consider that Einstein only used about 10 percent of his mental capacity and he was a genius. If he only used 10 percent, where does that leave you and me? Obviously we all have a lot of untapped grey matter, but does school or further education really prepare us for the "real world?" Yes, we may be taught skills or "how to" do something, but are we ever taught about the really important things, such as a positive mental attitude and principles such as sowing and reaping?

Are we taught that we create our own destiny by the thoughts we think? Unfortunately not. Instead we are taught that education will get us a safe, secure job. The problem with that is that safe, secure jobs don't exist anymore, and even if they did, they fail to realise that attitude is more important than education.

What's the point of being highly educated and having a lousy attitude? I'm not saying education isn't important— we all need to be educated— but a person with very little education and a positive attitude will go a lot further in life than a highly educated person with a negative attitude.

Thomas Edison (1847-1931), the man who invented the electric light bulb, was in school in Milan, Ohio, for only three months, but ironically he became very successful. Born into a poor family, by the age of fifteen he had published his own newspaper. Before he was twenty he had invented a vote recorder and a stock quotation printer. In 1876 he had his own laboratory, and this led to inventing the phonograph as well as the electric light bulb.

Albert Einstein (1879-1955), the man who received a doctorate and published his own Theory of Relativity, dropped out of school at age fifteen and was considered an "average student" by the time he left. He would often skip school in order to play the violin or study physics on his own.

These are two examples of people who became very successful despite having very little education.

Learning or acquiring wisdom is something that never stops. It starts from the day we are born and continues throughout our whole lives until we die. Only a fool would think otherwise.

As Edmund Hilary said, "It's not the mountain we conquer, but ourselves." Part of wisdom is also being teachable and being willing to humble yourself and ask for advice when necessary but also knowing who to seek advice from and who not to seek advice from. (This is covered later.)

The book of Proverbs has much to say on the subject of wisdom. *"Blessed is the man who finds wisdom, the man who gains understanding, for she is more profitable than silver, and yields better returns than gold. She is more precious than rubies, nothing you desire can compare with her. Long life is in her right hand; in her left hand are riches and honour. Her ways are pleasant ways and all her paths are peace. She is a tree of life to those who embrace her; those who lay hold of her will be blessed"* (Prov. 3:13-18).

Further benefits of wisdom are:

"My son, do not forget my teaching, but keep my commands in your heart, for they will prolong your life many years and bring you prosperity. Let love and faithfulness never leave you; bind them around your neck, write them on the tablet of your heart. Then you will win favour and a good name in the sight of God and man. Trust in the Lord with all your heart and lean not on your own understanding; in all your ways acknowledge him, and he will make your paths straight. Do not be wise in your own eyes, fear the Lord and shun evil. This will bring health to your body and nourishment to your bones. Honour the Lord with your wealth, with the first fruits of all your crops, then your barns will be filled to overflowing, and your vats will brim over with new wine. My son, do not despise the Lords discipline, and do not resent his rebuke,

because the Lord disciplines those he loves, as a father the son he delights in" (Prov. 3:1-12).

What could possibly compare with such words? While I'm sure we all want the rewards, how do we become wise, you might ask? How do we gain wisdom? We do it by learning from the wise. We do it by putting positive into our minds every day. But it's not just a case of putting positive in, we also need to be avoiding the negative at the same time. Both are vital if you want to be successful in life. I've never heard of anyone who became wise by reading newspapers or watching TV and I've never heard of anyone who became wise by hanging around with negative people who were going nowhere in life. But I do know many people who became successful in life by learning from people who were already successful. I know of many people who became successful be-cause they controlled what went into their minds on a daily basis.

Remember, there is a reason for everything and the reason you are where you are right now in life is because of your thinking. You could liken it to the law of cause and effect. For every effect there is a cause, and every cause has an effect. Your thinking is the cause and your life, at the moment is the effect. If you want to change your life (the effect) then you need to change the cause (your think-ing) .The law of cause and effect can apply to anything, not just your thinking. Here are some examples:

CAUSE	EFFECT
Politicians who put money be-fore the environment.	Global warming
Too much leniency in our law and order system	Increase in crime
Greed	Poverty
Generosity	Prosperity

Every effect can be traced back to a cause and every cause however big or small, will have a corresponding effect. This is because mother nature always has and always will seek balance. Whether we realise it or not, or believe it or not, our thinking determines the results in our lives. God didn't create some people to be successful and others to be failures. He created us ALL with the potential to be great. God gives us all potential, but then it's up to us to do something with it and develop that potential.

Don't Go with the Flow

Most people have heard the saying, "Just go with the flow," and that is just another way of saying, "Be average," or, "Follow the masses." But who wants to be average? If you want to be average then do what he average person does, think like the average person thinks and you'll have an average income and an average lifestyle. But if you want to be above average and have an above average lifestyle, you're going to have to develop some success habits instead.

The Bible warns us of the dangers of conforming to the world. It says, *"Do not conform any longer to the pattern of this world, but be transformed by the renewing of your mind"* (Rom. 12:2). And in the book of Matthew we are also reminded of the benefits of not conforming to the world and that a very small percentage of people are willing to make the changes required in order to become successful. *"Enter through the narrow gate. For wide is the gate and broad is the road that leads to destruction and many enter through it. But small is the gate and narrow the road that leads to life and only a few find it"* (Matt. 7:13-14).

That's why less than 5 percent of the population ever become truly successful; they are the only ones who are willing to pay the price. But what is the price, you might ask? Well, part of the price is being willing to change. Willing to change your habits and the way you think. Yes, hard work is part of the price in anything, but hard work alone won't do it. You've got to be willing to change. A lot of people are afraid of change and are afraid of what other people might think if they are classed as "different." Unfortunately these people don't usually get very far in life and end up conforming to the "masses." As a result, they end up with a similar lifestyle to the masses. I must admit that it does take a bit of courage to step outside your comfort zone and develop some new habits, but doesn't God command us to be courageous? Of course He does, and He also promises us that He will never leave us. *"Have I not commanded you? Be strong and courageous. Do not be terrified; do not be discouraged, for the Lord your God will be with you wherever you go"* (Josh. 1:9). And God always keeps His promises. In the whole of the Bible there has not failed one word (Josh. 23:14). That's because God's word is absolute and God's word is the truth.

The Myth of Brainwashing

Before we go any further, I would first like to explode a myth that has been around for some time. It's called the Myth of Brainwashing. I've heard people say it so many times, and I'm sure you've probably heard it too. But some people, when they hear you talking about positive thinking, say, "Sounds like a whole load of brainwashing to me." Well, my answer to that is they're right, but what they fail to realise is that everybody is brainwashed. People who say positive thinking is brainwashing are themselves brainwashed; only they don't realise it. It's not a question of "Are we brainwashed or not?" It's a question of "Are we brainwashed positively or negatively?" People who say that positive thinking is brainwashing are usually brainwashed negatively. They are brainwashed by TV, radio, and newspapers, and sometimes that is only the tip of the iceberg.

The reason we are all brainwashed is that no one's mind is ever blank. We are always thinking something. It's just a case of whether we are thinking positively or negatively. And what determines if we are thinking positively or negatively? Yes, you've guessed it. It is determined by we have allowed to go into our minds.

In fact everything has an effect on our minds. When we read something, it brainwashes us. When we hear someone else speak, it brainwashes us. If we watch TV, it brainwashes us. If we read a positive thinking book, it brainwashes us. When we associate with other people, they rub off on us, and consequently it brainwashes us. Every time we see an advertisement it brainwashes us. All day long we are all being brainwashed. When someone is brainwashed negatively they usually don't know why they are negative, they just see the world as a sad state of affairs. Only when you start to control what goes into your mind, do you realise the power and the effect sources of input have on your mind. In other words, you become aware, and only when you become aware do you become wise. I don't mean that we are wise in our own eyes but wise enough to control what goes into our minds on a daily basis.

Brainwashing is going on all around us all the time. If we cast our minds back to the 1930s, there was a lot of Nazi propaganda in Germany, especially in the schools. Children were being brainwashed and were being told what to think.

That was negative brainwashing like the history of the human race has never known. Even today, at a political level there is brainwashing going on. It's called "political correctness." Politicians who give the impression of doing good are actually telling people how to think. No person, whether they are a politician or not, has the right to tell you how to think or how to bring up your children, but it's going on. It's your birthright to be able to choose how to think. Be careful what you accept mentally and be careful what you allow into your mind. Does it violate God's word? There are some forms of brainwashing we should reject and there are other forms we should embrace. Which do you prefer, positive or negative brainwashing?

These 3 Things Will Change Your Life

At the beginning of this chapter I mentioned that this chapter was the crux of the book. Well, you are now at the crux of the chapter. Where you end up in life will be largely determined by these three things:

WHAT YOU LISTEN TO:-
Listen to a positive motivational CD for thirty minutes to one hour every single day.
WHAT YOU READ:-
Read for fifteen minutes from a positive thinking book every single day.
WHO YOU ASSOCIATE WITH:-
Associate with positive, successful people on a regular basis.

I have seen so many people's lives changed as a result of doing these three things. I have seen people who were unhappy become happy, people who were lacking confidence become confident, people who were looking for direction find purpose, people who were negative become positive, and people who were poor become wealthy. This doesn't mean that your problems will go away. Your problems will still be there, but you'll be able to handle them better. Remember, for these three things to work, you also need to be avoiding the negative at the same time, so that as far as possible you are allowing only positive into your mind. What would be the point of reading fifteen minutes from a positive thinking book and then reading a negative newspaper? Or what would be the point of listening to a motivational CD in your car and then coming home and switching on the TV or radio? You would neutralise all the good you had done. Please don't misunderstand me; I'm not suggesting that we stop listening to music. Of course we should still listen to music, as long as in the course of the day we also listen to something positive and motivational as well. Just as we spoke about controlled viewing regarding the TV we also need to practice controlled listening when we are in the car.

What You Listen To

When you are in the car, there is a choice of three different types of input. Two are positive and one is negative. The choice is music, something motivational, or the radio. You've probably already guessed that it's the radio that you need to avoid. Think about it, if the only two sources that you allow into your mind (in terms of listening) are uplifting music and motivational speakers, and all else is screened out, then your attitude is going to start to change because what goes in must come out. Although what we listen to is only part of the equation, it is vitally important nevertheless. Remember that when you listen to something, you are going to think about what you've just heard. In other words, you are allowing that person to occupy some of your mind. I don't know about you, but I'm particular who I let occupy my mind and I would prefer it to be occupied by thought of success and happiness. Listening to successful people speak will cause us to think thoughts of success and listening to uplifting music will help us to think thoughts of happiness. It's good that we have a combination of both.

The Bible tells us that whatever we listen to will have a multiplying effect: "Therefore consider carefully how you listen. Whoever has will be given more; whoever does not have, even what he thinks he has will be taken from him" (Luke 8:18). Even the music you listen to can uplift you or drag you down depending on what it is, so become aware of everything you listen to and check your emotions to see how it's making you feel.

One thing you cannot do is escape your own mind. All you can do is change what's in it. The reason we need to listen to something motivational every day is because motivation is not permanent. We could be extremely enthusiastic and excited one day, but if we fail to put anything positive into our minds the next day, our enthusiasm and excitement will very quickly fade and disappear. As Earl Nightingale said, "If we fail to plant thoughts in our minds, then our subconscious will feed of the random thoughts that reach it, as a result of our neglect." It's similar to the idea of keeping fit. Just because we may be as fit as a fiddle just now doesn't mean we are going to stay that way if we choose not to exercise any more. We can't expect to because physical fitness, like mental fitness, has to be constantly worked at and maintained. We never ever get to a point where we can stop— that's if you want to stay positive of course.

It's also important that you listen to something motivational for at least thirty minutes to one hour every day. Anything less than thirty minutes doesn't have much effect, so you need to make it a priority to fit it in somewhere during the course of the day. The initial reaction to this from most people is, "I don't have time to take thirty minutes to an hour out of my day to listen to a CD, I'm too busy!" And that's true, we are all busy. The good news is, you don't have to. We don't deliberately take time out to listen to a CD, but we listen to them while we are doing other things.

How many minutes do you spend driving in your car each day? When you're at home, what about the time you spend eating? You could be listening to something at the same time. What about the time you spend getting ready to go to work in the morning? You could also be listening to something while you are brushing your teeth or washing the dishes. It's amazing the amount of wasted time we have, and it's up to you how you fit it in. It doesn't have to be thirty minutes to an hour of constant listening. It can be broken up into different segments during the course of the day. For example, you may spend ten minutes listening to something motivational first thing in the morning while you are having breakfast, ten minutes in your car while driving to work, and ten minutes on the way home. Or you could decide to break it up into five minute segments. It really doesn't matter how you do it as long as, in the course of the day, you listen to something motivational for a minimum of thirty minutes in total.

Obviously the more the better, but that is up to you. Personally, I wouldn't have time either to take that amount of time out of my life every day just to listen to a CD, but because we work smarter instead of harder, we are able to fit it in.

As I've already mentioned, I think it's important that we don't just listen to motivational materials but also to uplifting music as well. We need to remember that life isn't just about work and mentally we need to switch off too. Just as in the case of physical exercise, where the times of rest in between the workouts are just as important as the workouts themselves, so are periods of listening to music, or maybe even silence, just as important as the motivational input. We don't want to burn ourselves out physically or mentally, so we need to keep a balance.

What You Read

Never underestimate the power of the written word. If reading isn't powerful then how has the Bible changed so many lives? Reading is food for the mind. Just as you wouldn't want to fill your physical body with greasy, fattening food every day, neither do you want to fill your mind with negative mind food every day either.

A lot of people take really good care of themselves physically but fail to take the same care of their minds. Remember the subconscious controls the body, not the other way about. Although what we listen to is powerful (classed as external motivation) reading goes right to the core of our being, and it changes us from the inside out. Realise that when you read something, it is immediately picked up by your subconscious and it changes your state of mind. This is true whether it's a positive thinking book, a newspaper, or anything at all for that matter. Whatever you put into your subconscious controls your life. Whatever you make a habit of reading, whether positive or negative, will affect your attitude, your outlook, and ultimately where you end up in life. Do you want doom and gloom from a newspaper to control your life, or do you want thoughts of success, happiness, and self-confidence to control your life instead? It's not a hard choice is it? That's if you want to become successful, of course. So guard your mind; it's your most valuable possession.

There's no such thing as standing still mentally. We are all changing all the time. We are either learning and growing (in a positive direction) or we are not using our brains as we should and are heading in a negative direction. There is no in between. The only thing to be decided is the direction in which we will go, but we will go in one direction or another. The good news is we choose the direction, by choosing what we read. What will you choose to read? What did you read today? What will you read tomorrow? Only you can make these choices.

The amazing thing about reading positive books is that it forces positive thoughts into our minds. Remember what we said in an earlier chapter, that positive and negative thoughts cannot occupy our minds at the same time? Well, guess what happens? That's right, the more we force the positive in, the more the negative gets shoved out. I must admit this is not an overnight process. To change a lifetime of negative habits, beliefs, or programming is a major undertaking and is going to take a bit of time to change. But it is more than worth the effort. When we read positive books, you could liken what happens in our minds to switching on the light in a room. The light and the darkness cannot co-exist. One or the other must dominate. When the light is off, the darkness dominates, but as soon as the light is switched on, the darkness disappears and the light dominates. You could look upon reading positive books as the light and the darkness as negative thoughts. Each time you read, you force the negative out and the positive dominates, but to do that you need to be reading for at least fifteen minutes every day. Yes, every day— that's if you want to be successful. I know this will be a stumbling block for a lot of people because usually you hear comments such as, "I don't like reading," or, "I've not got time to read." And I must be honest with you, it was a major stumbling block for me in the beginning, because I hated to read. But now, because I know what's in these books and the benefits that have come from reading positive books, I wouldn't even let one day go by without reading. Looking back, if I had known the life changing power of books I would have started reading a long time ago. Up until then I had probably been reading all kinds of negative junk, which had done nothing for me in my life, so I figured that these books would just be the same. How wrong I was, but at the time I didn't know that.

There was once a speaker at a seminar talking about reading for fifteen minutes a day, when someone in the audience said, "But I don't like reading," to which he replied, "Well, stay broke then." Obviously he didn't beat around the bush, but then again, his job was to tell people what they needed to hear, not necessarily what they wanted to hear. The purpose of this book is the same. Some people try to negotiate the price of success by picking and choosing the bits they like and leaving out the bits they don't like, such as reading. People who do that never succeed at anything because they are not willing to pay the price.

Realise that nothing worthwhile comes easy, and the secret to success is hidden in your daily routine. It's what you do every day that will determine where you end up in life. After all, what is the future except a whole collection of today's put together?

When you think about it, isn't fifteen minutes a day a very small price to pay if it's going to help us become successful? I personally think it's a very small price in comparison to the benefits which come from it. Henry Ford said, "Thinking is the hardest work there is, that's why so few people engage in it."

What do you want out of life? Are your dreams and your financial future not worth reading for fifteen minutes every day? People who say they don't have time to read are actually fooling themselves, because everyone has twenty-four hours a day. Successful people have twenty-four hours a day and unsuccessful people also have twenty-four hours a day. The difference is in what they do with their time.

Successful people have different priorities from unsuccessful people; that's why they're successful. Successful people make the time to read, whereas unsuccessful people don't. They may spend their time elsewhere such as watching TV or at the local bar, but somehow in some way they will still spend their twenty-four hours, only in a different way. At the end of the day, we all have to make our own choices and decide what we want out of life.

I place such a high priority on reading that, if I was to come home late at night after being out on the road and I was only going to get four hours sleep because I was up early for work in the morning, I would rather still read for fifteen minutes and get even less sleep rather than go straight to bed and get four hours sleep, no matter how tired I was. Quite a change for someone who used to hate reading! Some people may read more than fifteen minutes, and that's great, as long as you realise it's not so much the amount you read that's important but how often you read. How often you read is of vital importance. Some people think if they skip a day or two of reading, they can make up for it by reading a whole load (or the amount they have missed) a few days later. Well, they've missed the point, because the mind doesn't work that way. Any motivation we've had will have faded twenty-four hours later. If we're not reading something positive twenty-four hours later then the negative thinking will start to creep back in. Remember the example of the light and the darkness in the room? And that motivation is not permanent? That's why the secret to success is hidden in our daily routine. The positive input from reading has to be built on the positive input from the day before, to be truly effective. Our thoughts have a cumulative effect and tend to multiply based on our input from day to day.

Just as positive thoughts will multiply by reading positive books, so will negative thoughts start to multiply if we fail to put positive into our minds. Reading for fifteen minutes every day is far more beneficial than missing two or three days then reading for a few hours at once. There are actually two reasons for this. The first one we have just covered, but secondly, these are not ordinary books. Positive thinking books are not supposed to be read like novels. Why is this? Because they are teaching books and there is such a thing as information overload, which can be counterproductive.

Sometimes I read up to half an hour a day, but personally I wouldn't go above that because if you were reading that amount every day it would be ample information for your mind to work on a day-to-day basis. Your mind will absorb more (or a higher percentage) of fifteen to thirty minutes reading than it would by reading two or three hours at once. So we need to pace ourselves by reading a little bit every day rather than a whole lot now and again. We need to look upon the game of life as a marathon rather than a sprint.

It doesn't matter what time of day or night you read as long as it gets done. Some people like reading first thing in the morning and others prefer reading last thing at night, while some prefer to work through it during the course of the day.

It really doesn't matter when, but obviously based on your schedule, this is something you can choose to fit in any time you want. We also need to learn to make use of any downtime we have. This is time which is wasted through no fault of our own. For example, you may have a dentist appointment and find yourself sitting in the waiting room for half an hour with nothing to do. Or you may be on a long plane journey or waiting to catch a train and find out it's running an hour late. These are all opportunities to read. Obviously we want to speak to people around us too, but it's also an opportunity to do some reading at the same time. Why not keep a book in the car or carry one with you, especially if you are a busy person. That way you can make maximum use of any opportunities you get.

Some people complain about the cost of a book and say they can't afford it, but if they can't afford it, that's exactly why they need to buy it. I know that may sound a bit strange, but any kind of personal development tools such as books or CDs will, in the long run, help you to make more money so you need to look upon them as an investment, rather than a cost.

Two of the main differences between people who are broke and people who are wealthy is their thinking and their habits. Broke people will look upon buying personal development tools as a cost, while people who become wealthy look upon them as an investment. Different thinking resulting in different habits, resulting in a different lifestyle. The irony of the whole thing is that it's the books that change your thinking in the first place! You can't afford not to have them.

Even the Bible has something to say regarding this. *"Do not forsake wisdom, and she will protect you; love her, and she will watch over you. Wisdom is supreme; therefore get wisdom. Though it costs all you have, get understanding"* (Prov. 4:6-7).

I realise some people may genuinely not have as much money as other people. In that case you need to make it a priority, even if it means cutting back on something else. What is your future worth to you? How important are your dreams to you? Is it not worth paying out a little bit more just now so that you can make a whole lot more later on? Remember to think long term. That's another major difference between people who are broke and people who are wealthy. Broke people only think short term, whereas people who become wealthy think long term.

Even people on relatively low incomes usually find the money for things that are important to them, so a lot of the time it's a case of priorities rather than income. What's more important to you? Only you can decide that. But for the benefit of people who think they don't need to read, remember this truth:

YOU DON'T KNOW WHAT YOU DON'T KNOW.
YOU ONLY KNOW WHAT YOU KNOW.
THE MORE BOOKS YOU READ, THE MORE YOU KNOW.
THE MORE YOU KNOW, THE MORE YOU REALISE
YOU DON'T KNOW.
— Anonymous

The Power of Association

The people with whom you associate will probably have more influence over where you end up in life than any other single factor. If we like it or not or believe it or not, we become like the people with whom we associate. Obviously this can be good or bad, depending on who it is. How many times have you heard of children who were considered "good kids," suddenly getting into all kinds of trouble because they started to hang around with the wrong people? The fact of the matter is that people rub off on us and it is extremely powerful, especially to our subconscious mind. The way people think and the words they speak influence us. What they focus on and what they continually talk about has an effect on us. Their attitudes and opinions influence us, their habits and their behaviour influence us, and sooner or later, if we hang around with them long enough, we will start to think like them and become like them. Remember, all these things are continually picked up by your subconscious mind, which will eventually become your dominant way of thinking. People always tend to gravitate towards like minded people. The book of Proverbs also points out that *"He who walks with the wise grows wise, but a companion of fools suffers harm"* (Prov. 13:20).

Just as hanging around with negative people can cause us harm, we need to remember that some people can actually be a good influence in our lives too. As it says in the verse above "He who walks with the wise grows wise." Indicating that their wisdom will also rub off on us. We need to choose our friends and associates very carefully. But how do you know if someone is a good influence or not? There are probably many reasons, but I can think of a few positive character traits that I would look for, such as:

A PERSON WITH A POSITIVE MENTAL ATTITUDE
This is as essential to success as oxygen is to breathing.

A PERSON WITH INTEGRITY
Integrity is a must if you want to become wealthy.

A PERSON WHO ENCOURAGES YOU
This is essential. So many times I have seen people presented with an opportunity to better themselves and their so-called friends tried to talk them out of it or criticised them because they didn't want them to get ahead of them. A true friend will encourage you, not discourage you. They will build you up and never put you down.

A PERSON WHO USES POSITIVE WORDS
Not only is this an indicator of what type of person they are, but as already mentioned, it will have an effect on you.

A PERSON WHO LOOKS FOR THE GOOD IN OTHERS
So many times we come across people who gossip about other people or constantly look for faults in people. We need to avoid these people and associate instead with people who look for the good in others.

A PERSON WHO HAS THE LIFESTYLE YOU WANT
If you want to become successful, then you need to be associating with people who are already successful.

Remember, you become like the people you associate with. If your ambition was to make a million pounds a year, it would be a good idea to go to seminars where the people there were making at least a million pounds a year. There's a very good chance that if they have already done it themselves, they can teach you how to do the same. In other words, I wouldn't seek advice on becoming wealthy from someone making only ten thousand pounds a year. If they knew how to become wealthy, don't you think they would have already done it themselves? And if you do take their financial advice, there's a very good chance you might end up in the same financial situation. Before you get advice from someone, look at the fruit on the tree. In other words, whatever you are getting advice about— and this applies to anything, not just money— ask yourself, how successful is this person in this particular area? If they are successful in that particular area and you would also like to be in the same position, by all means listen to them and take their advice. But if they don't have the success you want in that particular area, don't listen to them. Instead go and seek advice from someone else who is successful in that particular area, and they can teach you how to do the same. The Bible also recognises the importance of this principle. *"Make a tree good and its fruit will be good, or make a tree bad and its fruit will be bad, for a tree is recognised by its fruit"* (Matt. 12:33).

Suppose you wanted advice about your marriage. Who would you listen to? Someone who had been divorced three or four times, or someone who was happily married and had never been divorced? Obviously the results speak for themselves, but it's amazing who people will take their advice from. People will take advice from their friends without even considering whether they have achieved in that area or not.

I know people who have been presented with amazing opportunities to enhance their lifestyle, but they allowed their "friends" to talk them out of it. Now, none of these "friends" were anywhere close to being financially independent, but they took their advice anyway. I'm not saying these people didn't mean well, but how good can their advice be if they haven't achieved themselves? A person's advice is only as good as their own achievements.

I remember one guy who turned down an opportunity to become financially independent and his reason was that although he was very interested in the idea, his father was a financial advisor and had advised him against it. Ironically, his father was not financially independent himself because he worked for a boss, yet he was advising him how to improve his financial situation. I don't say that to put down financial advisors, because I'm sure a lot of them are very good at what they do, but the point I want to make is this: it doesn't matter what title someone has or how much status they have, if they don't have the fruit on the tree, then why listen to them? *"A good tree cannot bear bad fruit, and a bad tree cannot bear good fruit"* (Matt. 7:18).

Some people go to the extreme. They either take everyone's advice or they take no one's advice. Both extremes are dangerous and can lead to failure. Sadly, today there are very few people who have your interest at heart, and even if they do, how good is their advice?

One of the great advantages of a good network marketing business is that the people who teach and train you have already achieved the success you want. They are not simply teaching a theory or something they've learned from a textbook but something they have already been through themselves.

This book is not about network marketing, but I think it is an excellent way of associating with positive, like-minded people on a regular basis. It also gives you the opportunity to learn and to be around people who are actively pursuing their goals. Any advice you get from the people in your line of sponsorship is going to be sound advice, because their success is built on your success. In other words, because of how the business is structured, they don't make any money until they've helped you make money first, which means they genuinely have your interest at heart. A good network marketing business also gives you access to purchasing positive thinking books and other motivational materials on an ongoing basis.

If you want to achieve greatly in life you need to first of all know what you want and, secondly, have a plan to achieve it. Sadly, a high percentage of people don't even know what they want, let alone have a plan to achieve it. As a result, these people tend to just drift aimlessly through life, never really getting what they want. How will you know if you've achieved your goal if you don't have one in the first place?

Another aspect of association which network marketing provides is mentorship. Mentorship is vitally important to your success, because we all need help and advice from time to time. We all need someone we can confide in and we can trust. This provides you with an excellent opportunity to get advice from someone who is where you want to be and has probably been through what you're going through.

The aspect of association doesn't always involve business. Depending on your religious views (if you have any) going to worship services not only provides you with the opportunity to worship Almighty God but also allows you to associate with like-minded people on a regular basis.

How you choose to associate with people is completely up to you. We are constantly associating with people each and every day no matter what we do. I have merely listed some examples which I personally have found extremely beneficial in my life, and in no way am I implying that you should do the same.

Sometimes we find ourselves in situations where there are negative people that we cannot avoid. There may be negative people at your place of work that you are forced to work with. This is a bit more awkward, because unlike other situations, you may not be able to just walk away, especially if that is your only source of income.

Unless you're planning to change jobs or become financially free so you don't have to work, all you can do is be the best you that you can be. We cannot control other people or what they do, but we can control ourselves by controlling what we put into our minds and by choosing how we respond. I believe the old saying is true, "We cannot change the wind, but we can adjust our sails" (Anonymous).

At times like this when you have to work with negative people, the system of putting positive into your mind every day becomes even more important, although we should be doing that anyway if we want to achieve our dreams and goals in life. As I've already mentioned, to get maximum benefit from this book (especially what's in this chapter) you need to be doing everything I've suggested simultaneously. Because they are so important I'll list them again:

1. WHAT YOU LISTEN TO
2. WHAT YOU READ
3. WHO YOU ASSOCIATE WITH

Any form of picking and choosing or trying to negotiate what we've just covered will severely limit your success and effectiveness. Remember, the problem is your thinking and the solution is your thinking. What are you thinking just now? Are you thinking, "That's not what I want to hear," or are you thinking, "That's what I'm going to do." Only you can decide that.

> "Fear not that your life will come to an end,
> but that it will never have a beginning."
> — Anonymous

The Solution (Part B)

The reason I have decided to split this chapter into two parts is because there are other things I consider are also vitally important to our success in life.

Our ability to effectively deal with people and get on well with them is a major part of being successful. We need to remember that people are important and we all need other people, directly or indirectly. Everyone plays a part in the game of life and we are all interdependent. Think about all the people we rely on from day to day. If our car needs repaired, we rely on mechanics to fix it. The new parts which are fitted had to be manufactured by someone. We rely on farmers to produce crops. We rely on the mailman to deliver our mail. If we are travelling by plane, we rely on airline pilots to get us safely to our destination. If we are unwell, we rely on doctors and nurses and trust them to do their job well. We rely on people who serve us at checkouts when we want to buy food. Our favourite clothes and furniture all had to be designed and manufactured by someone. The music we love listening to had to be produced by someone. If there is a fire, we rely on firemen to do their job and put it out. If there is a war, we rely on the armed forces to defend our country. If we are selling a product, we rely on customers to buy it, otherwise the product is useless. Whatever way you look at it, people are important. If you can master the art of making people feel important, this will go a long way toward increasing your effectiveness when dealing with other people.

So how do you make people feel important? You can do it in a number of ways, but here are some suggestions:

- Make eye contact and smile.
- Call people by name.
- Be first to say hello.
- Don't talk about yourself, but ask questions about them and listen.
- Talk less and listen more.
- Don't interrupt.
- Thank people and show appreciation.
- Give credit and praise when it's due.
- Focus on people's good points instead of their faults.
- If you can't say anything positive, don't say anything at all.

The Bible commands us to treat other people the same way that we would like to be treated ourselves, because ultimately the way we treat other people is how we will be treated. "A man reaps what he sows" (Gal. 6:7). The reason God commands us to treat other people well is not only because it's the right thing to do, but also for our own benefit because we will reap what we have sown. Think about it, how do you treat other people? How do other people treat you?

One of the major skills to master in the art of dealing with people is the ability to be a good listener. Some people think that the more talking they do, the better they are at conversing with other people, but actually the opposite is true. A good conversationalist listens at least twice as much as he talks. Remember, God gave us two ears and one mouth and we should use them in that proportion. *"He who answers before listening—that is his folly and his shame"* (Prov.18:13).

I suppose you've probably been in the same situation yourself when you've been sitting talking with some friends when suddenly someone bursts in the room in the middle of the conversation and immediately talks right over the other person at about twice the volume in order to command the attention. Not only is it bad manners, but indirectly what they're saying is, "What I've got to say is more important than what you've got to say." That's not the way to build good relationships.

We should always let other people finish talking before we start talking. Not only does this show respect for the other person, but it also gives us an opportunity to learn something. It's very hard to learn something while we are talking. Some people just can't wait to barge into the conversation. They may give the impression they are listening, but in actual fact they are not listening at all; they are thinking about what they want to say next and are just waiting for an opportunity to take over the conversation. When we listen to someone talk, we should really listen to what they are saying and we should also hear them out and let them finish before we start talking. Don't be too quick to speak; instead, practice listening more and learn to master the art of listening. Not only will you become more informed by listening, but this will win you more friends and increase your popularity.

By listening sincerely to what someone is saying, you are also making them feel important. The unspoken message that comes across is, "I'm taking the time to listen to you, so you must be important to me." When you do listen, give people your undivided attention. Stop whatever you are doing and look at them when you are listening to them. There's nothing worse than trying to talk to someone when they are doing something else and you know they're not really listening. For example, someone may be trying to tune in the TV and you've just asked them a question or told them something and they heard you but they're not really listening. They're probably not even looking at you while saying things like, "Is that right?" or, "Oh, really?" or, "My goodness," and they haven't even taken their eyes off the TV and are still tuning it in. Then once they've finished doing what they're doing, they turn round and say, "What was that?" and you have to repeat it all. Obviously it would be much better if they stopped doing what they were doing and gave you their undivided attention and looked at you. Either that, or if they were unable to stop, they could say, "I'm sorry, can you hold on for a few minutes?" and then give you their full attention once they had finished. That would be much better than pretending to listen but not.

Another important aspect of being a good conversationalist is to ask questions (and then listen, of course). Asking people questions, especially about themselves, shows that firstly, you are interested in them and secondly you care about them. Who do most people like to talk about? Who is everyone's favourite person? Yes, you've guessed it, THEMSELVES! One of the best books I have ever read regarding people skills is. 'How To Win Friends and Influence People' by Dale Carnegie, and I consider it a must-read for everyone who wants to master the art of dealing with people.

If we realise that people love to talk about themselves and their interests, rather than us and our interests, this will give us valuable insight into what kind of questions to ask in the first place. Remember, if you want to become successful in life, you need to stop being self-focused and become others-focused instead. We all need to change a few gears in our head from time to time. We can never expect any great measure of success unless we change our current way of thinking.

So what kind of questions should I ask people? you may be thinking. Well, there are two things to bear in mind when asking people questions if you want to be a good conversationalist.

1. Ask people questions about themselves and their interests.
2. Ask open-ended questions.

Let's look at number one. We've already mentioned the fact that people are primarily interested in themselves, not you. People love to talk about themselves and what's going on in their lives. For example, if you know someone who has just come back from holiday, you could say, "How was your holiday?" and they'll gladly tell you. That's a whole lot better than saying, "Hi, let me tell you about my holiday." Or if you knew someone who was a golfer, you could ask them if they've been playing any golf recently. A mistake a lot of people make is that they talk about their own interests instead. For example, suppose you liked football and the other person hated football. If you kept talking about football then you probably wouldn't be their favourite person. Subconsciously, they may even try to avoid you. You need to put your interests aside and become others-focused if you want to be popular.

Some people could talk for hours if you get on the right subject, and the interesting thing is, they do all the talking. You only asked a question, yet they still think of you as a great conversationalist because you allowed them to talk about themselves. When asking people questions, get in the habit of frequently using words such as 'you' and 'your' and avoid using 'I',' me',' my', and 'mine' as much as possible. As a result you will be well liked and you will win many friends.

Secondly, it is much better to ask open-ended questions rather than closed-ended questions. An open-ended question is one which requires people to elaborate rather than simply answer yes or no. For example, if you said to someone, "Are you the manager?" That requires a yes or no answer. But if you said, "How did you get involved in this line of work?" It requires people to elaborate and give you some information about themselves rather than just a simple one word answer. This also helps to keep the conversation going.

Thank People and Give Credit When It's Due

We also need to remember to thank people and praise them when they deserve it. Why is it that (especially in the workplace) when people do something extremely well no one says a word, but if they mess up or make a mistake then they hear all about it? It's all very well pulling people up for mistakes they've made in order to try to remedy the situation or correct their behaviour, but we should also place equal emphasis on giving credit and appreciation for a job well done. This is the difference between a good leader and a poor leader or a good manager and a bad manager. Remember, it's a well known psychological principle that whatever behaviour is rewarded will either continue or increase. Everyone loves positive recognition and people thrive on it. If you give praise and recognition when it's due, then people will perform just to please you.

This also gives people a feeling of value and makes them feel important. A major complaint in the workplace today is that people don't feel appreciated enough for their efforts. Some people feel as though they are just a number, like a small cog in a big wheel. This is usually the result of poor management.

This principle doesn't only apply to the workplace, it applies anywhere. It could be thanking a family member or a neighbour for doing you a favour or it could be as simple as thanking someone for delivering something to your door. Whatever it is, we should make it a point to thank them and show our appreciation. Another way of showing your appreciation is by giving people a tip. Obviously this is optional and is a personal choice, but it certainly shows appreciation and gratitude for what someone has done.

It's also a good idea to get in the habit of complimenting people when appropriate but the important thing to realise about giving compliments is that they must be genuine and sincere. Flattery or giving phony compliments is actually worse than giving none at all because people can see through it and they resent it. They may even think you are trying to manipulate them or have ulterior motives. True compliments come from the heart and actually benefit you as well as the recipient. Some people mistakenly think that if they give other people too many compliments then it will detract from their own self-image but actually the opposite is true. The more we build other people up, the better our own self-image becomes in the process. *"Therefore encourage one another and build each other up, just as in fact you are doing"* (1 Thes 5:11).

Focus on People's Good Points

It's so easy to focus on people's faults and what you don't like about them and many people do, but winners focus on people's good points and learn to overlook the faults. This doesn't mean that they don't face reality or that faults or problems don't exist but as far as possible they don't give any attention to them unless it is absolutely necessary. Winners also realise they themselves have faults, so why should they be critical of other people? The Bible clearly warns against judging others because we ourselves will be judged (Matt. 7:1-5). Apart from anything else, life isn't much fun if you're constantly looking for the bad in people. Why not focus on their good points instead? Occasionally you might hear someone say, "But I can't think of anything good about that person," and if you honestly can't think of anything good then it's better to say nothing rather than criticise them unnecessarily.

Some people are very quick to criticise other people, but I believe the old saying is true, "Never criticise someone until you've walked a mile in their shoes." The problem is that we assume things about other people. We think we know the full picture and we make judgments on them. The moment we do that, we are at fault, not them. Not only are we at fault for judging but also for assuming. We don't know what's going on in another person's life or what problems they face, so if we don't know the facts we shouldn't assume because most of the time we are wrong. This doesn't mean we should ignore someone's behaviour or let them off the hook but we do need to have a certain degree of tolerance.

Gossip is also a major human fault which is condemned in the Bible, although many people do it. Gossip doesn't usually achieve much and can cause a lot of trouble. Even if the person you are gossiping about isn't present, the person you are gossiping to will realise that when their back is turned you will probably gossip about them as well. In other words, if you are a gossip, you probably won't be very highly thought of by anyone. Remember, you reap what you sow and if you criticise other people you will reap criticism.

The book of Proverbs tells us, "He who guards his lips guards his life, but he who speaks rashly will come to ruin" (Prov. 13:3). Gossip can get us into all kinds of trouble, and I'm sure we're all guilty of saying things we regret and wish we hadn't said and as a result have got ourselves into some tricky situations. The trouble with gossip is that once you've said something, you can't take it back and if there are other gossips present then who knows where it might stop? Have you ever trusted someone with a secret and later on found out they had told someone? How did you feel? Not very pleased? Or has someone ever approached you and said, "Will you promise not to tell anyone because so and so told me a secret and I promised not to tell anyone." Well, that person is a gossip and is not to be trusted because if you told them a "secret" then the same thing would probably happen with you. *"A gossip betrays a confidence, but a trustworthy man keeps a secret"* (Prov. 11:13).

Some people almost make a career out of gossiping. They are constantly fishing around to see what the latest stories are and as soon as they find out, they spread it like wildfire. To tell such a person a secret would be similar to broadcasting it on a loudspeaker because guaranteed, a similar number of people would find out. People like that are the cause of many an argument and much trouble. Sometimes they actually get a perverted kind of satisfaction out of causing trouble. If they didn't get their daily dose of gossip, psychologically they would starve. The book of Proverbs says, *"Without wood, a fire goes out; without gossip a quarrel dies down"* (Prov. 26:20).

Beware of people who talk too much because such people can sometimes paint a negative picture of other people before you've even met them. I don't know what it is about human nature but why do we have a tendency to blindly believe whatever people tell us about other people? I don't know why but I just know that when someone tells us something about another person, it has a very powerful effect on us and we should always keep an open mind and make up our own minds about people.

A person with an immature mind will blindly accept or believe whatever they hear about another person. A person with a mature mind will question whether it is fact or opinion— Is there any evidence or proof to back this up?— and even then they won't judge but will treat the person as an individual based on their own perception of them. Although the Bible explains the consequences of gossip, we also need to remember God's promises for obedience. *"He who guards his mouth and his tongue keeps himself from calamity"* (Prov. 21:23).

We are also told, *"When a man's ways are pleasing to the Lord, he makes even his enemies live at peace with him"* (Prov. 16:7).

For our enemies to live at peace with us we need to be obeying God in every area of our lives, not only regarding the words we speak. There is no such thing as being partially faithful or partially obedient. Disobedience in any area is still disobedience to God and He will still reward us according to what our deeds deserve.

Vision

It's important that we see people as they can be, not just as they are. We all have the potential to be great. Even though none of us will ever reach our full potential, we are all still capable of becoming so much more than we are. Every one of us was born with the seeds of greatness in us and it's up to us to grow and develop those seeds. Winners see the potential in other people even when they can't see it for themselves. Winners also believe in other people even when they don't believe in themselves. Whereas losers only see people as they are instead of seeing them as they can be. Winners also have the ability to see things as they can be, not just as they are. They don't just look at their present surroundings, but they are also looking ahead and thinking ahead. In other words, they are thinking long term instead of short term.

For example, people who are creative have vision. They are in the habit of using their creative imagination to paint a mental picture of what something could look like, compared to what it is right now. A painter will see in his imagination what the finished picture looks like before he even starts. A person who buys and sells property will imagine how good the property could look before they even buy it. A person who writes a book visualises the finished product being read by millions of people before the book is complete. There are many ways in which people can have vision or the foresight to look ahead.

Winston Churchill was a man who had great vision. Before the Second World War broke out in 1939, Churchill could see the threat posed by Adolf Hitler to the rest of the world but no one would listen to him until it was almost too late. While other people may have been looking only at present surroundings, Churchill was looking ahead and could see the potential dangers even although we were not yet faced with them. When you have vision, there is no room for complacency. People who are complacent tend only to look at present surroundings, whereas people with vision not only see the present surroundings but also see potential situations as well. What is your vision for your life?

Spread Good News

People like you according to how you make them feel emotionally. People love to be around people who make them feel good and are fun to be around. Think about it, who do you like to be around the most? Why? What is it about them or what qualities do they have that appeals to you? There's a good chance a lot of it has to do with the words they speak. Now think about people that you don't like to be around. Why don't you like to be around them?

What is it about them that repels you? Well, there's also a good chance part of the reason may have to do with the words they speak. They may talk too much or they may constantly moan and complain. They may constantly criticise people or they may be simply be too loud. Or could it be that they seem to delight in spreading bad news, which consequently makes you feel bad emotionally.

I realise that sometimes it's necessary to tell bad news when it can't be avoided, but if it's not absolutely essential then why do it? What's the point? How will it make the other person feel? Good or bad? Will they be glad they've spoken to you or will they wish they hadn't met you? Did you uplift their spirits or did you leave them with a picture of doom and gloom? Remember, the words you speak are very powerful and not only affect you but also affect the people with whom you come in contact. You will be liked or disliked according to the words you speak. *"Pleasant words are a honey comb, sweet to the soul and healing to the bones"* (Prov. 16:24).

If you want to be well liked, you need to leave people feeling better after they've spoken to you than before you met them. The problem is that when you constantly focus on bad news, it becomes a habit. Your whole outlook and perspective on life seems to shift to one side. The upside is that focusing on good news can also become a habit if you choose to do so. Attitude and focus is a choice and always will be.

Someone once said that a truly successful person with a positive mental attitude could've just had a disaster and you wouldn't know it. Yet what do most people do? They just can't wait to let everyone know.

We spoke earlier about how the subconscious mind associates things with other things. Well, people associate us with the words we speak and they also associate us with how we make them feel. It doesn't take people long to mentally put together a picture of us and decide whether we fall into the category of "liked" or "disliked." The last thing you want is for people to be subconsciously avoiding you because of the words you speak. Why not decide today to focus on what's good and to speak only about what's good. You'll be a lot happier in the process and you'll have a lot more friends.

CHAPTER SEVEN

Money

"A generous man will prosper; he who refreshes others will himself be refreshed."

— Proverbs 11:25

Many people have different attitudes and beliefs about money. Some people believe money is scarce, while others believe money is plentiful. Some people believe there is some divine virtue in poverty, while others believe it is good to be rich. Regardless of a person's view, money is something we all need in order to survive. Whatever your beliefs are, the first thing we need to ask ourselves is, what actually is money?

Money is simply a medium of exchange. Money in and of itself is neither good nor bad. It can be used to do a lot of good or it can be used for evil. It's true that evil people use money for evil purposes, and do evil things for money but the money itself is not evil. Money is actually neutral. The same money could be used to buy food for people who are dying of starvation. One of the most misquoted verses in the Bible is when people say (wrongly) that money is the root of all evil, which gives the impression that money is evil. But how can money be evil? How can a wad of paper or a pile of metal coins be evil? Paper and metal by themselves can do no harm. It's people who are evil, by their attitudes toward money. The correct Bible verse however, is "For the love of money is a root of all kinds of evil" (1 Timothy 6:10). Notice how God is condemning the attitude and not the actual money itself. There is a big difference.

It is not a sin to have money, but it is a sin to love money. There are many Bible verses that give warning to the rich, but there are also many verses telling us that God wants us to prosper. For example, in the book of Matthew it says, *"It is hard for a rich man to enter the kingdom of heaven. Again I tell you, it is easier for a camel to go through the eye of a needle than for a rich man to enter the Kingdom of Heaven"* (Matt. 19:23-24).

Whereas we are also told, *"You will be made rich in every way so that you can be generous on every occasion"* (2 Cor. 9:11), and in Deuteronomy we are told, *"But remember the Lord your God for it is he who gives you the ability to produce wealth"* (Deut. 8:18). We must realise that if it was wrong to be rich then God would never have said that. So how are we to interpret all this? Is it mixed messages? Not at all. God is far too wise to do that, and Scripture will never contradict Scripture. Personally, I believe it is to do with priorities and attitudes. There are many things more important than money, but sometimes people get their priorities wrong. Some people who get rich get so wrapped up in their own desires that they forsake God in the process. Others place a higher importance on money than they do on people and consequently go against God's word as a result.

I believe that one of the reasons God warns us about being rich is because of temptation. This does not mean that every person who becomes rich will fall into temptation and ruin but there are many who do. The Bible says *"People who want to get rich fall into temptation and a trap and into many foolish and harmful desires that plunge men into ruin and destruction"* (1 Tim 6: 9). How many times have we heard of famous people who were rich coming to ruin or destruction because they were either tempted or got caught up in foolish desires? They may have had everything going for them and were extremely wealthy but made some bad choices and ended up losing everything in the process. But is that the fault of the money or the fault of the individual? Of course it's the fault of the individual because people make choices and every person will make different choices. Money cannot make a decision; therefore, it cannot be the fault of the money. If it was the fault of the money then every rich person would come to ruin and destruction, and that's not true.

There are many extremely wealthy people who are very generous with their money and use it for good purposes. Some people believe that if you are a Christian then you shouldn't have much money but my question to them would be, how much is too much? At what point when you make a certain amount of money does it become wrong? This usually leaves people with some blank looks because nowhere in the Bible does it say that once you make over a certain amount of money it becomes wrong. What God will judge us on is what we do with our money. It's very important that we understand the difference. God wants us to prosper, but He also wants us to glorify Him by using it for good purposes. He also commands us to give back a tenth of everything we make by giving to people less fortunate than ourselves. This is what the Bible refers to as tithing.

If we are fully obeying God's commands, then there is no limit to the amount of money we can make. Unfortunately, not everyone will obey God's commands because with money comes increased temptation and a tendency to cast God aside. This is what I believe God is warning against. *"For whoever wants to save his life will lose it, but whoever loses his life for me will find it. What good will it be for a man if he gains the whole world, yet forfeits his soul?"* (Matt. 16:25-26).

I can only speak from my own point of view and what has helped me but I found that there was a certain order of priorities regarding money, and if I violated the order then not only did I run into difficulties but I wasn't a very happy person either. If I kept the priorities in the correct order and never violated the order then things ran much more smoothly, I had less problems and I was a much happier person in the process. This was the order:

1. God
2. People
3. Money

This doesn't mean that money should be the third most important thing in your life because there are many other things which are far more important than money. For example, I'm sure we all place a far higher value on our physical health than we do on any amount of money, and I'm sure that peace of mind is more important to us than money. Money should never become more important than God or people, and this should be reflected in our daily lives. It's true that money alone won't make you happy. Happiness has to come from within and cannot be bought. Money alone is not success as some people might think, but it is a by-product of success. In other words, as a result of doing the right things, money will come automatically. The same can be said of happiness, which is also a by-product of success. If you go out to pursue happiness, you will probably never find it, but as a result of doing the right things and doing what you enjoy doing, you will be happy.

Money controls the choices we have in life and determines the quality of our lifestyle. Although money isn't everything, it is a vitally important commodity in our lives. With more money we have more choices, but without it we are extremely limited. When people who are critical of money say, "Money won't make you happy," they're right, but we need to remember that poverty certainly won't make us happy either. Just imagine what you would do if you couldn't keep up your mortgage payments and your house was going to get repossessed. Or if you wanted to travel abroad with your friends but didn't have the money or if you wanted to take time off work but couldn't afford to. How would you feel then? Do you think money is important to you? Of course money is important! If money isn't important then why do the majority of the population spend a major part of their lives working for it?

Believe it or not, some people who are critical of money actually spend a lot of their time working for money. I know it sounds crazy, but it's true. In fact, some people who criticise money actually buy lottery tickets as well. They wouldn't be trying to win money would they? These same people may criticise someone who gets rich through their own efforts yet they try to get rich without any effort. Is that not the love of money? It has been my experience that the people who love money the most are people who are broke. Because they haven't got much money they tend to put an even higher priority on money and material possessions than the rich do. Loving money has nothing to do with how much money you have, but it has everything to do with your priorities and your attitude towards it. The "acid test" to see whether you love money or not is not what you say but what you do with your money.

The Bible also warns us against getting rich quickly. *"An inheritance quickly gained at the beginning will not be blessed at the end"* (Prov. 20:21). That's why we see so many people who win the lottery, either lose it all in a relatively short period of time or get themselves into all kinds of difficulties as a result. The truth is that becoming wealthy is a process and has got a lot to do with your self-image. If all of the money in the world was divided up evenly, within a relatively short period of time (probably less than a year) most of the money would be back in the hands of the original people. Why is this? The reason is that successful people think differently, have different attitudes and habits than unsuccessful people, and as a result, they would have no problem becoming wealthy again. Whereas if we take for example someone who had a poor self-image, a negative attitude, bad spending habits, and believed it was wrong to be rich, it wouldn't matter how much money you gave them, it would be gone in a relatively short period of time. Why?

Because they received something for nothing. The inner person was still exactly the same; their habits, beliefs and attitude were still the same. As a result, this would be expressed physically in terms of situations, conditions, and events. So, true success is not measured by how much money you make but by **who** you become along the way.

Although a lot of people are critical of the rich, we need to remember that economically, the rich are the backbone of society. They provide jobs, goods, and services that we as a nation could not function without. For example, someone who starts up a business and becomes wealthy may end up providing jobs for hundreds or thousands of people. If there were no rich, then who would lend you money if you wanted to buy a house? If there were no rich, who would manufacture your dream car or your favourite clothes? Someone has to own the company. People who criticise the rich don't realise that when someone gets rich everyone benefits. To put it another way, a rich person will benefit the country a lot more than a poor person will. This doesn't mean that they are a better person, not in the slightest, but instead of being a drag on society, they actually contribute something instead. And when someone gets rich, they will also pay more tax, which in turn, benefits the country.

The Bible commands us to give a tenth of our income to people less fortunate than ourselves, so let's take for an example a man called Fred who makes £200 per week. Because he is extremely charitable, he gives a tenth of his income to the poor, which is of course, £20 per week. Then one day Fred goes into business for himself and after a few years he is making £2000 per week, and because he is extremely generous he is still giving a tenth of his income to the poor, which is now £200 per week. So because Fred has become better off financially, instead of giving away £20 per week, he is now able to give away £200 per week, or more if he wants. If Fred was still poor then he wouldn't be able to help as many people as he can just now. One of the reasons that you need to become rich is so you can help more people. Remember, the poor can't help the poor, and as it says in the Bible, *"Can a blind man lead a blind man? Will they not both fall into a pit?"* (Luke 6:39).

Usually the first thing people say when they hear that is, "But not everybody will be that generous," which is true. And my question to them would be, "Is that the fault of the money or the fault of the individual?" Of course it's the fault of the individual, so why blame the money? We are all given free will, and if an individual chooses to do evil with their money instead of good, no one is responsible but them.

As long as there is poverty in the world, and unfortunately there always will be (despite what politicians might say about making poverty history), people who have money have a responsibility to help people who are less fortunate than themselves. *"There will always be poor people in the land. Therefore I command you to be open-handed toward your brothers and towards the poor and needy in your land"* (Deut. 15:11).

Please don't confuse this with giving money to the government. What I'm talking about is charitable giving and not taxation, which is a completely different issue. Even if the rich were taxed at the same percentage as everyone else, they would still pay far more in tax than the poor or the middle class because it's a percentage, so why raise the percentage?

Is it not better to reward someone for succeeding rather than penalise them? Should we not encourage people to succeed rather than discourage them? Bear in mind that when the rich are taxed at a higher percentage, it's not the poor who get the money, it's the government. That's why socialism is a backward form of government. There is no incentive to succeed because the more successful you become, the more you are taxed. Why not give more incentives to people who want to succeed and less incentive to people who don't want to succeed?

The more handouts people get, the less incentive they have to succeed because they're getting something for nothing. Is there not something wrong with the system when a person who is out of work and living on government benefits says, "It wouldn't be worth my while working because I would be making less money," and indirectly it is the rich and the producers in life who are paying for it. Yet these same people may be critical of the rich. It's far better to be giving someone a hand up instead of a handout. As long as you're giving people handouts, then they're more likely to stay in that position because they become dependent instead of independent. The best way to help another person is to help him to help himself. The Chinese proverb says, "Give a man a fish and you feed him for a day, but teach a man to fish and he can feed himself for a lifetime."

To become successful you need to take responsibility for yourself and for creating your own future. Some people wonder why the rich get richer and the poor get poorer. It has nothing to do with good luck or bad luck as some might suggest, but it has everything to do with their thinking and their habits. As previously mentioned, the rich think differently from the masses and they have different habits, therefore they have different results in their lives. It's the law of cause and effect in action. The cause is their thinking and the effect is wealth (in the case of the rich). Unfortunately the same principle holds true for poverty. For example, one person might believe it is good to be wealthy while another believes it is wrong to be wealthy. One person might choose to be an employee while another chooses to start their own business. One person might have a positive attitude while another has a negative attitude. One person might be generous while another might be greedy. One person may have integrity while another does not. One person may control their emotions while another does not. One person may spend less than they make while another gets into serious debt. The list could go on and on, but as long as people think differently and have different habits, and they always will, then there will always be a gap between rich and poor. The good news is that you are in control of your choices and therefore in control of your destiny.

The Bible says that whoever has the feeling of wealth, more wealth will be added. Therefore the opposite must also hold true; poverty thinking will only lead to more poverty. In either case it becomes a self-perpetuating cycle. It will either be an upward spiral to wealth or a downward spiral to poverty. If you want to attract more of the same, just keep doing what you're doing. The only way to break out of the poverty cycle and into the wealth cycle is by striking at the root cause, which is your thinking and your habits. Positive habits give you the feeling of wealth while negative habits give you the feeling of poverty.

Obviously, if you change your habits, then everything else changes accordingly. Incidentally, this is not a book about financial advice because I am not a financial advisor, but it is intended to help explain the principles of money. If you want to change your financial situation, you won't do it by simply changing your conscious thinking; you need to go deeper than that and change what's in your subconscious mind. Remember, it is your subconscious that attracts situations, conditions, and events, not the conscious.

Negative Cycle

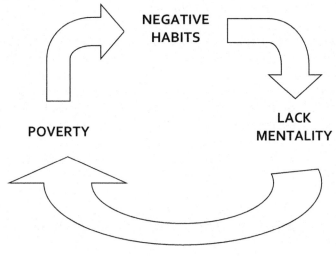

Positive Cycle:

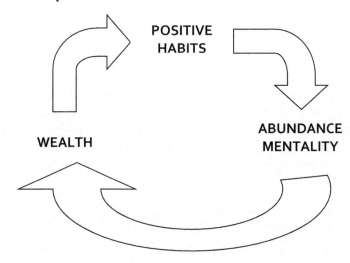

So how do I change what's in the subconscious, you might ask? How do I break out of the poverty cycle and into the wealth cycle? Well, firstly, I would recommend changing what goes into your mind on a daily basis (as we covered in Chapter 6: The Solution), and secondly, I would recommend changing your habits, because your habits will determine what goes on in your mind. (Remember, actions speak louder than words, especially to your subconscious.).

You may or may not have heard of the 70/30 rule. Once again I take absolutely no credit for this, but only wish to pass on what I have been fortunate enough to learn from other people. The 70/30 rule by itself won't necessarily make you wealthy, but it will turn your financial situation around and set you up for wealth by putting you in a positive cycle. If you want to achieve great wealth then you also need to have a plan to create wealth, as well as following the 70/30 rule. For example, suppose a person working a day job for a boss decided to put into practice the 70/30 rule (changing their habits) and they also started their own part-time business (a plan to create wealth). This person could become extremely wealthy, as a result of making those two decisions. The 70/30 rule simply means this:

SAVE. 10%
GIVE. 10%
INVEST. 10%
And live off the remaining 70%.

I realise you may be thinking what I first thought when I seen that, and I thought there's no way I can do that, I'm toiling to live off 100 percent just now. But don't be too quick to condemn it. Why not give it a try first? You'll probably be amazed at how well you can cope. Why not try it for a year and, if you don't feel it's been beneficial, you can always revert back to your previous habits? Remember, if you do what average people do then you'll end up with what average people have. If you want your life to change then you need to make a few changes in your life.

People who become wealthy also use different words from average people. For example, the average person might say, "I can't afford it," but someone who becomes wealthy says, "I'll find a way to afford it." The average person says," "I'll never be rich," but someone who becomes wealthy says, "I'm getting richer and richer." The average person says, "It's too expensive," but someone who becomes wealthy says, "It's all relative." Can you see the difference between the two extremely different types of thinking leading to two different types of results? One person has an abundance mentality, while the other has a poverty mentality. Remember, every time you repeat a statement such as, "I can't afford it," you are programming your subconscious mind to make sure it becomes a reality, and it will keep you broke!

If you are in debt then you may want to seek financial advice or read books on getting out of debt before going any further. If you don't think you could manage to live off 70 percent of your income then you may want to read books on money management and financial literacy in order to find out in what areas of your life you can cut back. It's amazing the amount of things we spend our money on that we could easily get by without. You may have to re-arrange your priorities or make a few sacrifices, but what's your financial future worth to you?

Save 10 Percent

Wouldn't you agree that it's not how much you make that's important but how much you keep? What's the point of having a high salary if you have nothing left over to show for it? You'll just be broke at a higher level. Even when someone gets a pay increase, you'll often find that they don't have any more money left over than before. This is because most people live beyond their means. Many people actually spend more than they make and get themselves into debt.

One of the keys to becoming wealthy is to spend less than you make, and one way to do this is by saving 10 percent of your total income. You may be good at paying your bills and paying other people, but why not pay yourself as well? By saving 10 percent, not only are you putting something away for a rainy day but you also have interest working for you instead of against you.

A high percentage of the population have credit card debt and are making repayments on loans. As a result these people have interest working against them, eating away at their financial well-being. Why not make interest a friend instead of an enemy? This is just one of the differences between the rich and poor. Some people say, "But if there's anything left over I always save it." Well, they've missed the point. You need to pay yourself before paying the bills, not afterwards. You may have to do a bit of juggling, but it's worth it. A book I strongly recommend is 'The Richest Man in Babylon' by George S. Clason, and in his book he explains about the multiplying effect of saving regularly and how we can benefit from the effect compounding interest. He also makes it clear that we should not save less than 10 percent, and he also found that when he started saving he seemed to attract more money. Could this have anything to do with developing a "wealth mentality?" Someone who saves money will have more of a wealth mentality than someone who doesn't save. Habits create your mentality. Your mentality then creates or attracts the physical equivalent. This is a very important principle, but is seldom understood, especially by the masses.

It's also a good idea to have a separate account for savings only. You may have many other transactions going on in other accounts, but this one needs to be kept separate. That way you can clearly see progress being made, and the only time you should take money out is for absolute necessities. Try to get into the habit of living off 70 percent of your income, so that even if you do have a lot of bills to pay, this account will still continue to grow.

Give 10 Percent

The Bible refers to giving a tenth of our income to people less fortunate than ourselves as "Tithing," and this is the standard by which we will be judged. It's not so much the actual amount given that's important to God, but the percentage. We are told: *"From everyone who has been given much, much will be demanded; and from the one who has been entrusted with much, much more will be asked "* (Luke 12:48).

Remember, it's all His anyway, and He only asks us to give back a tenth of what's already His.

The reason God commands us to give a tenth is not only because it's the right thing to do but also for our own benefit, so that we ourselves can prosper. Many people have a hard time believing how this can be true because the natural tendency is to think that if we give something away, we will end up with less. I know it isn't logical, and to some it may even sound crazy, but if you want to improve your financial situation, the best thing you can do is give some of your income away. The Bible tells us that it is possible to give and become richer. *"Honour the Lord with your wealth, with the first fruits of all your crops: then your barns will be filled to overflowing and your vats will brim over with new wine"* (Prov. 3:9-10). "Give and it will be given to you. A good measure pressed down, shaken together and running over, will be poured into your lap. For the measure you use, it will be measured to you"

(Luke 6:38). I must admit that I myself had a hard time believing how this principle could be true, but it is. I thought, how can you possibly give something away and end up with more? But remember this truth:

Whatever you give you receive.
Whatever you share multiplies.
Whatever you withhold diminishes.
Whatever you lust after, you lack.

That's why the Bible says, *"A generous man will prosper"* (Prov.11:25). Some people think that the more money they hold on to, the more they will end up with, but not only is this an untruth, it is also an illusion. Remember, the devil is a trickster and a liar, and he wants to keep you broke. God is the Way, the Truth, and the Life, and He wants you to prosper. But some people might not trust God's principles and think that they won't work. If you don't think you could manage to give a tenth, at least give something, and you can always increase it gradually. But remember: *"Whoever sows sparingly will also reap sparingly, and whoever sows generously will also reap generously"* (2 Cor. 9:6).

Bear in mind the effect that giving also has upon your subconscious mind. Remember, we spoke earlier about the wealth cycle and poverty cycle, and that different thinking creates different results? For example, if a person believed that money was scarce (lack mentality) then that's exactly what they would see manifested in their life. Whereas a person who believed money was abundant (wealth mentality) would see abundance manifested in their life. Each time you give money away, you create an abundance mentality. The message your subconscious mind receives is, "He must be rich because he's giving it away," which in turn gives you the feeling of wealth. Whereas if a person gave nothing away, that would create a "lack mentality," and the message their subconscious mind would receive is, "He's obviously broke because he's giving nothing away," which in turn would give them the feeling of poverty. Two extremely different habits and two extremely different messages to your subconscious mind, producing two extremely different results.

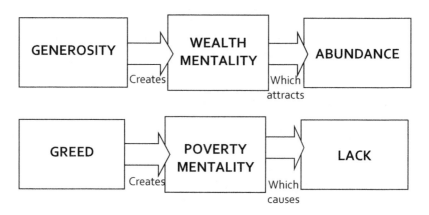

Remember, God will do more with the 90 percent than any of us could ever do in a million years with 100 percent, because the 90 percent that's left over multiplies. None of us can ever out give God, He will always give us far more back than we can ever give Him. If we don't give a tenth, then we are robbing God. In the book of Malachi, God actually challenges us to test Him in this principle, and God is never going to be made a liar. "But you ask, 'How do we rob you?' "In tithes and offerings. You are under a curse— the whole nation of you— because you are robbing me. Bring the whole tithe into the storehouse, that there may be food in my house. Test me in this*," says the Lord Almighty, and see if I will not throw open the floodgates of Heaven and pour out so much blessing that you will not have room enough for it"* (Mal. 3:8-10).

Although the benefits of giving are tremendous, God also warns us about the consequences of not giving. The Bible says, *"He who gives to the poor will lack nothing, but he who closes his eyes to them receives many curses"* (Prov. 28:27). God also warns us that our giving must be done in private. In the book of Mathew we are told, *" Be careful not to do your acts of righteousness before men, to be seen by them. If you do, you will have no reward from your Father in Heaven. So when you give to the needy, do not announce it with trumpets as the hypocrites do in the synagogues and on the streets, to be honoured by men. I tell you the truth; they have received their reward in full. But when you give to the needy, do not let your left hand know what your right hand is doing, so that your giving may be in secret. Then your Father, who sees what is done in secret, will reward you"* (Matt. 6:1-4).

Invest 10 Percent

As I am not a financial advisor, I won't even attempt to give you financial advice, but it is important that you set aside this 10 percent in order to create some kind of investment for your financial future. If you want financial advice, I strongly recommend you read some of Robert Kiyosaki's books (The Rich Dad Series). Books such as Rich Dad, Poor Dad and the Cashflow Quadrant are excellent books to start off with. But what I will say, and I'm sure many business professionals will agree, is that the best investment you can ever make is to invest in yourself. By that I mean, commit to an ongoing personal development program (similar to what was discussed in Chapter 6: "The Solution").

If you are going to commit to a personal development program then you are going to need money to buy books, CDs, and to pay for seminars. Some people may grumble about this, but if you want to become successful, then there's a price to be paid.

Remember, investing means that you have to give first, before you get anything back. You may not see any immediate return, but successful people always think long term. They know that the money and the effort they put in just now will eventually pay off and that the payoff is always greater than the price they paid. Not everyone understands this principle or is willing to pay the price because many people only think short term. Losers and people who want to get rich quick think that if they don't see an immediate return, then it can't be any good. The Bible says, *"A sluggard does not plough in season; so at harvest time he looks but finds nothing"* (Prov. 20:4).

Be assured that success will never attack you. You will never become successful simply by wishing or hoping. You have to pay a price, and if you don't pay it you fail; it's as simple as that. It may be harder for an employee to grasp this principle than a business owner because an employee has a different way of thinking. This doesn't mean that a business owner is a better person, but an employee is used to getting paid as they go along, whereas a business owner may have had to put out a lot of money and effort first, before they reaped any kind of financial reward for their efforts. So if you are an employee just now and you want to become wealthy, you need to develop "business ownership mentality" while still working your job. The only way to do that is by changing what goes into your mind on a daily basis.

Passive Income Versus Active Income

If you are working hard for money and everything you earn is based solely on your own efforts, then your chances of becoming wealthy are greatly reduced because there is a limit to how much work that you, personally can do in a day. Unfortunately, in school you are only trained to look for a job. There is little if anything taught about business ownership or investing. As a result, the majority of people spend their whole lives working hard for money. One of the differences between the rich and the poor is that the rich don't work for money, they have their money working for them (or other people working for them as the case may be). For example, a person may hold their wealth in real estate so that not only are they receiving rental income, but the property is also increasing in value at the same time. In other words, their money is working for them.

The difference between passive income and active income is that active income is income that comes in only as a result of you physically trading your time for money. In other words, if you don't go to work, you don't get paid. Passive income is income that comes in and continues to keep coming in, regardless if you work again or not. Of course, you will have to put in some effort initially to set it up, but once it's set up, it will continue to provide you with a steady stream of income for years and years. This also frees up a lot of your time to do more important things or to pursue your dreams and goals. Here are some examples of passive income:

ROYALTY INCOME	As a result of writing books, making records, inventing things, and income from network marketing business, etc.
DIVIDENDS	Paid to shareholders.
RENTAL INCOME	From Property.
INTEREST	On Savings.

Although these are just a few examples, if you want to have time and money freedom, you need to have sources of passive income instead of just working hard for money. You may work hard for money your whole life and you may be making good money, but you'll never have the time to go with it. One without the other isn't much good.

The only way to achieve your dreams and live the lifestyle you want is to create multiple streams of passive income which do not require you to go to work every day, thereby giving you the time to go with it. This can never be achieved by working for a boss. What Robert Kiyosaki explains in his books is that, even if you do work for a boss and you are trading time for money, learn to convert active income into passive income. For example, a person working a day job may decide to use some of their income as a down payment on a rental property. The house may have been purchased with active income, but it now provides a steady source of passive income. The beauty of passive income is that it can be developed on top of what you already do without affecting your current source of income.

Self-employed people can sometimes fall into the category of trading time for money if they are operating as a one-man business.

Unless they expand their business and are leveraging their time through other people's efforts, they will be limited to what they can personally do in a day. John Paul Getty said, "I would rather have 1 percent of 100 people's efforts than 100 percent of my own effort."

One principle that the rich use that the poor do not is the power of leverage. That is exactly the principle upon which network marketing businesses are built. The richest people in the world have two things in common: Firstly, they are all in business for themselves. Secondly, they all leverage their time.

Too many people today are "time poor." They may be making good money, but they are caught up in the 9-to-5 rat race. They are so busy making a living that they don't have a life. Sometimes we get so wrapped up in the "how-to" that we forget "why" we are working. Instead of our work being a means to an end (which is our dreams), it becomes an end in itself.

Sadly, this is the way it is for many people today, but it doesn't have to stay that way and it's never too late to change. Remember, time is more valuable than money. If you lose some money, you can always make some more, but once you lose time it's gone forever. Life is not a dress rehearsal. This is it! When you get to the end of your life you cannot press rewind. Why not go for your dreams? Why not start today?

CHAPTER EIGHT

Persistence

"Blessed is the man who perseveres under trial because when he has stood the test, he will receive the crown of life that God has promised to those who love him."

— James 1:12

Without persistence everything else is futile because this is the one character trait upon which everything else is built. Unfortunately, lack of persistence is common to the majority of people. Many people begin many things but few ever finish. But before we go any further, let's first take a look at failure, because believe it or not, failure is a major part of success. Contrary to what some people believe, without failure there could be no success. This is usually a result of what they've been taught, either at school or by their parents. Some people are brought up to think that they should never fail or that it's something to be ashamed of. Nothing could be further from the truth. The mistakes we make that we learn from are the most valuable teachers we will ever have. It's only through failing that we learn what not to do and what to avoid. If we are wise, we will learn from our mistakes and take corrective action. Only if we make the same mistakes over and over does it become stupidity. Each time you fail, you become wiser and there is something to be learned. Someone once said that if you learn from a defeat then you haven't really lost. I'll be the first person to admit that failure and defeat are painful and some are more painful than others but here's what I found: The bigger and more painful the defeat the more important and valuable the lesson. Without learning these particular lessons, there's no way we could become successful. These painful lessons then become part of our character and our roadmap to success— as long as we persist.

Sometimes when we fail, the corrective action only requires a minor adjustment to get us back on track. It can sometimes be the little difference that makes the big difference. At other times, a major change is required. In war, military commanders constantly change their tactics to adapt to the changing situations. One example is the Allied bombing campaign over Germany in World War Two. While the Royal Air Force bombed at night, the U.S. Air Force bombed by day. In order to protect the American bombers from attack, they were escorted by long range fighters because at that stage in the war flying over Germany during daylight without fighter escort was almost suicidal. At first the fighters flew alongside the bombers, which may have been good for morale but according to one fighter pilot, was "bad for tactics." The reason being, when the German fighters made their attack it all happened so fast that although the American fighters responded quickly, some bombers had already been lost and the damage was already done. One American fighter pilot said that on one occasion they found themselves sandwiched between the bombers and the oncoming Luftwaffe. The Germans knocked out fifty-two bombers in about three minutes, so the American air chiefs changed tactics. Up until then the number one priority for the fighters was to protect the bombers but now the priority became "destroy the Luftwaffe."

Instead of flying alongside the bombers, the fighters would now fly way ahead of the bombers to engage the Luftwaffe before they could even get near the bombers. As the war progressed, the Allied fighters also began targeting the German fighters on the ground before they could even take off. This change in tactics turned out to be a war winning strategy.

It has been said that experience is the best teacher and I agree. No theory or any kind of knowledge can ever compete with experience. Paradoxically, the only way to gain experience is through trial and error. For example, an experienced cyclist at some point in their life had to learn how to ride a bicycle. They had to learn by making mistakes and falling off occasionally until they became good at it. There was no other way to learn except through trial and error. Could they possibly have learned to ride a bicycle by some other means? For example, by reading text books or getting advice, so as to avoid the painful experience of falling off? No, not at all because failure is an essential part of success.

You will normally find that the most successful people have also been the biggest failures. It took Thomas Edison ten thousand attempts to invent the electric light bulb but was he a failure? Not at all. Did he view himself as a failure even although he had failed thousands of times? Not at all, although many other people might have. The truth is, he was actually becoming successful. Each time he failed, he learned what didn't work and came a bit closer to success. With each failure he was also wiser. When asked if he felt like a failure because he had failed so many times, he replied, "I have not failed. I have merely found ten thousand ways which didn't work." The only time you fail is when you give up and quit. As long as you persist and keep taking corrective action, you are on the road to success.

What do you think the average person would have done? How many people would have given up after a dozen attempts or even fifty attempts? They might have been forgiven for thinking, "This is hopeless; it doesn't work," and quitting. But that's exactly what separates average people from successful people; their perception of and response to failure. Average people quit while successful people persist. Average people can't handle failure but successful people learn from failure and take corrective action. You need to change the way you view failure. Instead of being frustrated or disheartened, you need to ask yourself, What's the lesson to be learned here? What corrective action do I need to take? And then persist. There is also a big difference in attitude between average people and successful people. The average person says, "I'll give it a try," but successful people say, "I'll do whatever it takes." In other words, they don't give up until they get there.

The problem with saying, "I'll give it a try" is that it gives you an escape route when the going gets tough. That's not what winners do and that's not how they think. Winners burn their bridges so that there's no going back.

A good example of this was on D-Day (The Allied invasion of Normandy on June 6 1944). Although it was inevitable that there was going to be tremendous casualties and loss of life, they had to press on regardless. Once the command had been given for the huge invasion fleet to depart, there was no going back. No matter how severe the weather got, how much enemy fire they came under or how gruesome the situation was, the invasion was on. Quitting was not an option. There were only two ways out, and that was death or victory.

Edmund Hilary, the first person to conquer Mount Everest did not succeed on his first attempt, but was he a failure? Not at all, because he persisted until he did succeed. Before he succeeded he was actually reported to have stood at the bottom of Mount Everest shaking his fist at it and saying, "You can't get any bigger but I can." With that winning attitude and determination he was able to triumph over something which had previously defeated him.

Your ability to persist is in direct proportion to the size of your dream. The bigger your dream or your desire, the more unstoppable you become. I'm sure you've probably heard true accounts of people who performed amazing feats which, under normal circumstances would not have been able to perform. For example, the person who single-handedly lifted up a car to free a loved one who was trapped underneath it. Under normal circumstances, had they tried to lift it, they would not have been able to budge it. So why were they able to lift it on one occasion and not on another? The car weighed exactly the same, they were the same person with the same body, so what made the difference? The difference was desire. On one occasion the desire to free a loved one was so great that there was no thought in their mind of "not being able to" or, "What if I can't?" The only thought was, "Get them out," and so they did. I still don't know where we get our strength from at times like that but I just know that it's available to every one of us. When the desire is strong enough nothing will stand in our way.

In short, desire performs the impossible. How big is your dream? Is it big enough to keep you going when disappointment and fear threaten to steal your dream? Is it big enough to keep you going when there no longer seems any point carrying on?

Viktor Frankl, a psychiatrist who survived the Nazi concentration camps said that if a person has a strong enough "why," they can deal with almost any "how." He also said that the Nazis could take away your freedom, your dignity, and even your life, but as long as you were living, there was one thing that they could not take away. He referred to this as the last of the human freedoms; the ability to choose your attitude in a given set of circumstances. Our attitude is the one thing over which we have 100 percent control. Hopefully we will never have to go through what he went through but one thing is certain and that is, if we want to become successful we will be faced with adversity and pain. It's not so much what happens but how we respond to the pain that determines whether we become successful or not. It's human nature to shy away from pain and a lot of people do, but only a small percentage of people choose to endure and pay the price. That's why only a small percentage of people ever live a lifestyle that other people only dream about.

When Jesus was in the Garden of Gethsemane shortly before being crucified, He sweated blood because He experienced fear and pain just like us. He asked God the Father if it was possible that there might be another way. *"My Father, if it is possible, may this cup be taken from me. Yet not as I will, but as you will"* (Matt. 26:39).

When Jesus was on the cross, He was taunted by the people who were crucifying Him. They said, "If you really are the Son of God why don't you come down from that cross?" Someone else said, "He saved other people but He can't save Himself." Even the robbers on either side of Him threw insults at Him. We all know Jesus could have come down from the cross anytime He wanted to but instead He endured for our sake.

I want you to think about it. If Jesus done that for us, what excuse have we got for quitting? There is no excuse. I know this may not be of much comfort to you, but our struggles are necessary. Just as failure is a necessary part of success, so are our struggles an essential part of who we become. The bigger the struggle, the bigger the person it's going to make you. In the Bible, we are called on to persevere: *"So do not throw away your confidence; it will be richly rewarded. You need to persevere so that when you have done the will of God, you will receive what he has promised. For in just a very little while, He who is coming will come and will not delay. But my righteous one will live by faith. And if he shrinks back, I will not be pleased with him"* (Heb. 10:35-38).

The crucifixion was God's gift to us. What we do with our lives is our gift to God. What will you do with yours?

Strength Through Struggle

Contrary to what some people believe, not only are struggles necessary as part of our personal development but they also strengthen us. The harder the struggle, the stronger we become. There is no way of bypassing the struggles in order to become successful. Even if you could somehow bypass the struggles, you would not have gained the experience and strength of character required for success. It is only in the actual struggle itself that this can be found. Viktor Frankl, the man who survived the Nazi death camps, said, "That which does not kill you makes you stronger." Napoleon also said that the greatest single attribute of a soldier is not courage, as one might expect, but endurance.

The problem is that when we are going through the pain of adversity, we cannot see any benefit to our suffering. Sometimes everything seems to go wrong at once. The problem which once seemed major, now pales in insignificance to what now confronts us.

Disappointments, setbacks, fear, and anxiety all threaten to overwhelm us. The situation looks hopeless, and you may even start to doubt whether you were meant to do this. You may be thinking what I once thought: Where are you, God? I've asked you and asked you for help and there's no answer. In fact things are worse now than they were several months ago. Can't you hear me? I remember thinking these exact same thoughts several years ago, and what was one of the most difficult times in my life turned out to be not only a turning point, but a blessing in disguise. The benefits which came as a result of those struggles were far greater than the pain of the struggle.

Napoleon Hill said that within every adversity, setback, or disappointment lies the seed of greater or equal benefit. The problem is that we cannot usually see the benefit at the time, so we end up quitting. Sometimes the benefit does not become apparent until a long time after the struggle is over, but the irony of the whole thing is that many people never ever get to that point because they quit. I'm firmly convinced that if people could somehow see the benefits God has in store for them, they would persist. Persistence not only requires stamina but faith. You need to have faith in yourself and your abilities. You need to have faith that things are going to get better because they will, and you need to have faith in God's promises, because the Bible also tells us, *"Let us not become weary in doing good, for at the proper time we will reap a harvest if we do not give up"* (Gal. 6:9).

Notice how God says "at the proper time." Timing is very important regarding success because sometimes we think we are ready and we're not. God isn't going to give us anything we are not yet prepared for or couldn't handle. He wants to give us what He has in store for us but we must be ready. The problem is that sometimes we are convinced we are ready and we get angry at God when He doesn't give us the success right now. We need to trust His judgment rather than our own judgment. After all, who knows best? Us or our Creator? Too many of us think short term instead of long term. If success doesn't happen quickly enough then we bail out. We need to realise that anything worthwhile doesn't happen quickly and that the timing is different for everyone because everyone's situation is unique. It will happen for you if you persist, but you need to trust God and His perfect timing.

God Is Watching

Sometimes when we think we are ready for success and the success doesn't happen when we think it should, it can be for reasons beyond our understanding. Not only do we get despondent, but we can also become confused. We think God has forgotten about us or that He doesn't care, and we may even be tempted to think that success is only meant for other people. This is the work of the devil. Remember, the devil is a trickster and a liar and loves to plant the seeds of doubt in your mind in order to sabotage your success. The truth is, God is watching! He is watching to see if you really have faith in Him and His promises. He also knows that only in the deep valleys where character is forged, do we gain the strength to become successful. Although we may have already experienced a lot of pain, God sometimes allows us to experience further pain if there are lessons we have not yet learned. To some people this may not sound like the work of a loving God, but remember, if God was to give us the success we crave without being fully prepared, not only would the success be short-lived but He would be hurting us more than helping us. You could liken it to putting a soldier out on the battlefield without any armour or ammunition. What chance would he have? It's because God loves us that He allows us to experience pain. When the lessons are finally learned, we eventually break through to a new level of success. It's true that God sometimes teaches us through adversity because only then do we become more teachable and willing to make the necessary changes.

The struggle is different for everyone, depending on your self-image and your previous experiences in life. The worse your self-image, the more pain you will probably have to go through to get where you want to be in life. You will still get there, but it may take a bit longer. Don't compare yourself to other people. Remember, you are not in competition with anyone but yourself. It doesn't matter if the other guy succeeded before you, just as long as you get there—that's what counts!

When You Hit Rock Bottom, Keep Going!

Every successful person at some point hits rock bottom. Rock bottom is the place where the vast majority of people quit. Rock bottom is not a fun place to be, but there is no alternative but to go through it because your dreams are on the other side. Rock bottom is when you are so low that you cannot get any lower. Almost everything imaginable has gone wrong and it seems like there is no longer any point carrying on. You could be forgiven for thinking, "I knew it was going to be tough, but not this tough!" Disappointment after disappointment, failure after failure, and what do I get? Nothing! There seems to be no point in your suffering and you've almost given up on your dream. May I just say that at that point, you had better know what your dream is or you will quit because your dream is a major key to your ability to persist. That's what will keep you going.

Take comfort in the fact that when you are at rock bottom, eventually things have to get better because the only way you can go from rock bottom is up. Eventually something has to give. It will either be you or the obstacle. If you decide you are going to persist no matter what, then eventually the obstacle will start to give. But how long does rock bottom last, you might ask? I don't know how long it will be because rock bottom is different for everyone. I didn't know how long rock bottom would last for me; I just had to go on faith that things would get better, and they did.

I'll be honest with you, "rock bottom" almost sunk me. Looking back, it was a very thin thread of hope and my dream that kept me going. Not only that, but I thought "If I do quit, what am I going to go back to? Am I going to live the rest of my life being a quitter and forever haunted by thoughts of what might have been? Or am I going to persist?" I figured that the pain of regret would be worse than the pain I was going through. Not only that, but I knew eventually what I was going through would pass but the pain of regret would be with me forever. I remembered the words of Shakespeare, "This too shall pass," and the words of Christopher Columbus, "This day we sailed on."

The Comfort Zone

You will find many common character traits among successful people, usually the first and foremost being a positive mental attitude. One thing common to every single one of them is that they made it a habit to keep getting out of their comfort zone on a regular basis. Successful people know that success can never be found inside the comfort zone. Only mediocrity can be found there. This is where the vast majority of the population live. Is it then any surprise that the vast majority of the population never achieve their dreams or even come close to being the person they were capable of becoming? The comfort zone is responsible for stealing more people's dreams and robbing them of their potential than you could possibly imagine.

The comfort zone will also keep you broke. There is not much pain in the comfort zone but there are not many benefits either. The comfort zone is a place of conformity where people follow each other and dare not rock the boat for fear of rejection or ridicule. Only those who dare to step out of the comfort zone and risk defeat ever achieve greatly in life. As someone once put it, "You need to go out on a limb, that's where the fruit is."

God wants us to come as close to reaching our potential as possible. Although we will never reach our full potential, we are all capable of becoming so much more than we are. There's only one problem, something stands between us and what we could potentially become: the emotion of fear.

Fear is what stops most people from getting out of their comfort zone and taking a leap of faith. Getting out of our comfort zone not only involves taking advantage of opportunities but also developing new habits— for example, speaking to people you might not normally speak to or being first to say hello. When you are first to speak then you are risking rejection, but rejection is something you need to get used to if you want to become successful. Average people fear rejection; successful people embrace it. Even if you do get rejected, so what! It's not life threatening; you just simply move on and speak to someone else. Little by little, you begin to be able to handle rejection. Not that you will always be rejected— but when you are, you may be emotionally knocked down but not knocked out. You learn to pick yourself back up and dust yourself off.

It's a psychological fact that if you have fear of something and you are exposed to it long enough, then the fear begins to diminish. There is no other way to overcome fear but to continually do what you are afraid to do. Winners have learned to make a habit out of doing what's uncomfortable. When you do the uncomfortable long enough, eventually something interesting happens. The uncomfortable becomes comfortable and you create a new comfort zone. Now that you have experienced a higher way of living, what once used to be a comfort zone would now be very uncomfortable to go back to and you have no desire to go back to it. For example, a caterpillar has to leave behind the security of its cocoon in order to become a butterfly. It cannot experience being able to fly while still holding on to the comfort it once had in its cocoon. It has to let go. A baby has to leave behind the security of its mother's womb if it is to experience life. But if you could somehow communicate to the baby while it was in the womb, and tried to persuade it to come out, what do you think it would say? Well, because it doesn't know any better, the chances are that probably nothing in the world could convince it to come out because of the security it has in the womb. But isn't life far better outside the womb? Of course it is! We know that now, only because we are out. There's no way we could have known that while we were still in the womb because we have nothing to compare it to.

So it is with our comfort zones. If we have spent most of our lives there, then we may be reluctant or unwilling to step out at all. But the only way to get what we want out of life is by stepping out.

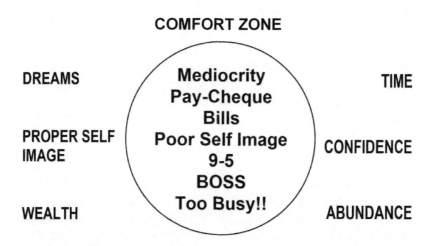

COMFORT ZONE

DREAMS

Mediocrity
Pay-Cheque
Bills
Poor Self Image
9-5
BOSS
Too Busy!!

TIME

PROPER SELF IMAGE

CONFIDENCE

WEALTH

ABUNDANCE

Very often, when we see someone successful, whether it is on TV or a speaker on a stage, we only see the finished product. We assume that because they are so confident just now, they were always like that. Or we may think that because they look so good just now, it must have been easy for them, or they've had a bit of luck or something.

Nothing could be further from the truth. What we don't see is the years of hard work and discipline that they had to put in to get there. We don't see the pain, the suffering, and years of sacrifice which contributed to their success. We don't see the failures, the defeats, and the times when they almost quit. We don't see the tears and the painful emotions they experienced along the way. But just because we didn't see them doesn't mean it didn't happen.

You could liken it to buying a brand new car. When you buy it, it looks beautiful, glamorous, and so appealing. But it wasn't always like that. At one point it was raw material and a pile of nuts and bolts. It certainly wouldn't have looked anything special then, although you would have been looking at the exact same material only in a different form. The only difference is that the finished product has gone through a process. Without the process there can be no glamour, and so it is with our lives. If we want to become successful, we have to go through a process, and the only way to go through the process is by getting out of our comfort zones.

What Might Have Been

The Bible tells us that every man shall give account of himself. (Rom. 14:12) Imagine when our earthly lives are over and suppose God shows us a movie of our lives. He questions us about certain things and asks us why we did or didn't do certain things. Now suppose He shows us a second movie entitled 'What Might Have Been' and we see the lives we could have lived if only we had stepped out of our comfort zones and taken some risks. We see the success we could have had if we had been willing to face our fears and trust in Him. We see the amount of people we could have helped if only we had persisted instead of giving up. We see the lives of others that we could have influenced as a result of our own success. In short, we wish we had persisted but it's too late. Will we see such a movie? Who knows? Maybe, maybe not. But we all have one thing in our favour, and that is time. The "What Might Have Been" movie is still within our grasp.

The truth is that we are the biggest stealers of our own dreams, not other people. We end up having internal dialogues with ourselves and talking ourselves out of our own dreams. If we are not putting something positive into our minds every day, then faith and hope can easily give way to fear and doubt. When that happens, we usually quit. Realise that when you quit, it is your decision and no one else can make that decision for you. Either way, success or failure, you decide.

I honestly believe that as we persevere, not only does God reveal more of Himself to us but He also reveals things to us that would otherwise have remained hidden. There's a big difference between simply believing in God and actually knowing Him, but only through obedience do we got to know Him. It is possible to develop a personal relationship with God where we are in constant communication with Him. The book of Revelation says, *"To him who overcomes, I will give some of the hidden manna. I will also give him a white stone with a new name written on it, known only to him who receives it"* (Rev. 2:17).

God wants to be our Partner in success. He will help us through the tough times and will never let us down. He will help us when we are afraid and guide us when we are confused and is available twenty-four hours a day.

He understands the pain we are going through because he Himself suffered pain. *"He holds victory in store for the upright, and He is a shield to those whose walk is blameless"* (Prov. 2:7)

Just as it is important to persevere, we also need to guard against complacency. There is a tendency to sometimes take it easy when we are winning, and believe it or not, we can actually do the same when we are losing. When we are losing, we sometimes get so frustrated or disappointed that we take a break. Unfortunately, some of these "breaks" become permanent for some people. So we need to keep full momentum from start to finish (if there ever was a finish!) We need to maintain our momentum whether we are going through good times or bad times. I must admit this is easier said than done, but with the help of motivational input and focusing on your dream, it can be done. The majority of people who quit do so when they are going through their toughest times, but as someone once said, "If you're going through hell, don't stop there!" If you stop there, you're going to be stuck there! Keep going and you'll eventually get through it.

Just for the sake of an example, imagine you were going on a train journey and the destination was your dreams, but there were many other stations along the way. Places such as Mediocre and Average and Hell. These were just a few of many potential stops. The only difference is that wherever you choose to stop, you're going to spend the rest of your life there. Where would you get off the train? Would you get off when you were going through some of the worst places you could imagine or would you stay on until you arrived at your dreams?

It's amazing the amount of people who choose to get off before reaching their dreams and spend the rest of their lives at some other destination. Ironically, Hell usually seems to be the last destination just before reaching our dreams.

It's almost as if we are being tested to see if we are strong

163

enough to handle success. Many are tempted to get off the train here and many people do. But it is only by going through Hell and refusing to get off that gives us the very strength we require.

Many people who choose to get off while going through Hell had absolutely no idea how close they were to the next station, which is their dreams. They couldn't see it because they were in the fog of adversity and therefore assumed it either didn't exist or was much further away than they had thought. Only those who endure and stay on until they reach their dreams experience the thrill of overcoming and the rewards that go with it. This is where winners can get off the train and enjoy the fruits of their labour. They know that they deserve success, because they know the price they paid to get there.

Finally, I'd just like to share a few words by Theodore Roosevelt.

"It's not the critic who counts; not the man who points out how the strong man stumbles, or where the doer of deed could have done better. The credit belongs to the man who is actually in the arena... who at best, knows in the end the triumph of great achievement, and who, at worst, if he fails, at least fails while daring greatly. So that his place will never be with those cold timid souls who know neither victory or defeat."

CHAPTER NINE

Stay Awake!

"I, the Lord, search the heart and examine the mind, to reward a man according to his conduct, according to what his deeds deserve."

— Jeremiah 17:10

At first I hesitated to include this chapter, but because of the changing times we are living in, I thought it was necessary to include it.

Today we are living in a world with mixed-up priorities and Christianity seems to be becoming less and less popular, if popular at all, especially amongst politicians. The problem is that we as a nation have fallen asleep. When I say fallen asleep, I mean lost sight of what's right and wrong. Much of what is wrong is now considered acceptable, and much of what is right is now frowned upon (such as God's word). We need to remember we are only on this planet for a short time, and compared to eternity, it is an extremely short time. What we do with our lives here on earth will determine where we spend our eternity. There's nothing wrong with success or becoming wealthy as long as we are obeying God and remember that He is the ultimate Owner and we are only managers over what He has given us. He has also left us an instruction book called the Bible. Everything we need to know regarding how to live our lives successfully is in the Bible.

This is also the Standard by which we will be judged, not necessarily the standards of politicians. The reason I say that is because today many of our politician's standards go against the Word of God, and many people have been deceived by these standards. For example, some politicians believe in banning the cross or banning the Bible, and they'll have a very convincing "reason" for doing so.

We see laws that favour criminals instead of the victim, and the excuse for that is usually "human rights" but the reality is more like human rights for criminals and little, if any, rights for the victim. The title "political correctness" may sound attractive to some, but the reality is loss of freedom of speech. Notice how the reality is very different from what these things are intended to portray (deception).

The Bible tells us that teachers of law and people in positions of authority will be judged more strictly than others. We are also warned that many false teachers will appear and give the impression of doing good. *"And no wonder, for Satan himself masquerades as an angel of light. It is not surprising then, if his servants masquerade as servants of righteousness"* (2 Cor. 11:14-15).

We also see "religious compromise" and moves towards a one world religion, which is in fact no religion. Politicians can come up with all types of excuses for banning the cross and banning the Bible, but in the book of Mark it says, *"If anyone is ashamed of me and my words in this adulterous and sinful generation, the Son of Man will be ashamed of him when he comes in his Father's glory with the holy angels"* (Mark 8:38).

As far as Christianity goes, there is no such thing as sitting on the fence or any kind of compromise. God makes it clear, *"He who is not with me is against me"* (Matt. 12:30).

Take for example the case of a homeowner who gets burgled in his own home, tries to defend himself and his family against an attacker and ends up getting prosecuted for it. Is that crazy or what? Does it encourage crime? Of course it does. Is it justice? What justice? So what does the Bible say about such a fiasco? The book of Proverbs tells us, *"Acquitting the guilty and condemning the innocent— the Lord detests them both"* (Prov. 17:-15).

The bedrock of any society is its constitution. A country can only be as strong as its constitution. The Bible talks about building your house on rock rather than on sand, as in the case of the wise and foolish builders. But some politicians are building their (or I should say our) constitution on sand. Nothing that's built on sand will long endure. *"Unless the Lord builds the house, its builders labour in vain"* (Psalm 127:1).

I believe God tries to protect us, but I also believe His protection is linked to our obedience to Him, not only individually but also as a nation. He died for us because He loves us, but if we forsake Him and His commandments then why should He give us the same protection? I believe God certainly helped us during the Second World War, when the odds were stacked so massively against us. As powerful as the Nazi war machine was, I believe that Hitler was doomed from the very start because he had built his house on sand.

In the book of Leviticus, when talking about punishment for disobedience, it says, *"I will lay waste the land, so that your enemies who live there will be appalled. I will scatter you among the nations and will draw out my sword and pursue you. Your land will be laid waste, and your cities will lie in ruins"* (Lev. 26:32-33).

One thing about God is that He always keeps his promises. We can count 100 percent on His word because it is the truth.

The Myth about Christians

Being a Christian does not make you a better person than anyone else, although some people have bought into the myth that supports this belief. Whether some Christians hold that view or not, is not the purpose of this chapter. The truth is we are all sinners like everyone else, "For all have sinned and fall short of the glory of God" (Rom. 3:23). You may be tempted to think that because someone is a follower of God they will be wise enough not to be deceived by some of our politicians. Not true.

The Bible tells us that even some of God's own followers will be deceived. *"For false Christ's and false prophets will appear and perform great signs and miracles to deceive even the elect - if that were possible"* (Matt. 24:24).

We need to stay awake and remember that our politicians' standards aren't necessarily God's. I'm not saying that all our laws are against God, but there are certainly more now than in the past few decades.

Such Things Must Happen

One day Christ is going to return, but here's the catch: no one knows when He is going to return. The Bible tells us it will be at the end of the three and a half year reign by the Antichrist. *"No one knows about that day or hour, not even the angels in heaven, nor the Son, but only the Father"* (Matt. 24:36). Suppose you were going to die next week. Would that change how you live your life today? The Bible tells us that some of us will not even taste death before He returns. He will come back to judge the living and the dead. *"Therefore keep watch, because you do not know on what day your Lord will come. But understand this. If the owner of the house had known at what time of night the thief was coming, he would have kept watch and would not have let his house be broken into. So you also must be ready, because the Son of Man will come at an hour when you do not expect him"* (Matt. 24:42-44). The Bible only tells us that He is coming soon, and of course, soon could be anytime. The only kind of indication we get is when the disciples ask him, *"When will this happen, and what will be the sign of your coming and of the end of the age?" Jesus answered, "Watch out that no one deceives you. For many will come in my name, claiming, I am the Christ and will deceive many. You will hear of wars and rumours of wars, but see to it that you are not alarmed. Such things must happen, but the end is still to come. Nation will rise against nation, and kingdom against kingdom. There will be famines and earthquakes in various places. All these are the beginning of birth pains"* (Matt. 24:4-8).

We are told in verse 33, *"When you see all these things, you know that it is near, right at the door."* This doesn't mean that we should be alarmed or live our lives in fear. In fact I believe the opposite is true. God still wants us to enjoy ourselves and live our lives to the full, but at the same time He is also warning us to stay awake! It is never too late to repent, and there is nothing God wouldn't forgive if we decide to change our ways and follow Him.

God is waiting for us with open arms. He wants us to come to Him. The Bible tells us *"Rejoice with me; I have found my lost sheep. I tell you that in the same way there will be more rejoicing in Heaven over one sinner who repents than over ninety-nine righteous persons who do not need to repent"* (Luke 15:6-7).

It is beyond our imagination what God has prepared for those who love Him. *"Listen, I tell you a mystery. We will not all sleep, but we will all be changed— in a flash, in the twinkling of an eye, at the last trumpet. For the trumpet will sound, the dead will be raised imperishable, and we will be changed."* (1 Cor. 15:51-52).

"Where, O death, is your victory?
Where, O death, is your sting?" (verse 55)

"No longer will there be any curse. The throne of God and of the Lamb will be in the city, and his servants will serve him. They will see his face, and his name will be on their foreheads. There will be no more night. They will not need the light of a lamp or the

light of the sun, for the Lord God will give them light. And they will reign forever and ever" (Rev. 22:3-5).

May God bless you on your journey of life, and may all your dreams come true.

I sincerely hope you have enjoyed this book. If you have, would you be please be kind enough to leave a review on Amazon.com or Shieldcrest.co.uk website? Or both if you wish. Many thanks.

ABOUT THE AUTHOR

Andy Holligan is an independent business owner in his native Scotland, Great Britain. He became involved in multi level marketing in 1995, which he worked part-time. The sales and training system changed his life- way beyond his expectations and he became a Christian in 1999.

What Holligan has written about in his books is based not on 'classroom theory', but on his own personal experience over a period of years. His hope is that other people might avoid the pitfalls he fell into and at the same time, benefit from what he has experienced. Please visit his website at:

www.solutionstoyourlife.com

Other Books by Andy Holligan

Printed in Great Britain
by Amazon

42884211R00099